FRIENDS DON'T LET FRIENDS DRIVE NAKED

KATHERINE BOWERS

SCRIPTORIA

an imprint of Sunbury Press, Inc.
Mechanicsburg, PA USA

an imprint of Sunbury Press, Inc.
Mechanicsburg, PA USA

For information about special discounts for bulk purchases, please contact Sunbury Press Orders Dept. at (855) 338-8359 or orders@sunburypress.com.

To request one of our authors for speaking engagements or book signings, please contact Sunbury Press Publicity Dept. at publicity@sunburypress.com.

FIRST SCRIPTORIA PRESS EDITION: September 2024

Set in Adobe Garamond Pro | Interior design by Crystal Devine | Cover by Victoria Mitchell | Edited by Gabrielle Kirk.

Publisher's Cataloging-in-Publication Data
Names: Bowers, Katherine, author.
Title: Friends don't let friends drive naked / Katherine Bowers.
Description: First trade paperback edition. | Mechanicsburg, PA : Scriptoria Press, 2024.
Summary: Navigating life's road can be daunting, like standing on the shoulder, fearing reckless drivers. But when we focus on God's faithfulness, detours become opportunities. He turns collisions, detours, and potholes into blessings on our journey." Buckle up!
Identifiers: ISBN : 979-8-88819-220-7 (softcover).
Subjects: RELIGION / Christian Living / Inspirational | RELIGION / Christian Living / Spiritual Growth | HUMOR / Topic / Religion.

Designed in the USA
0 1 1 2 3 5 8 13 21 34 55

For the Love of Books!

To my loving, encouraging and supportive daughter, Michelle.
I'll love you forever!

CONTENTS

Foreword   vii

Preface   xi

Chapter One: All Hat No Cattle   1

Chapter Two: Don't Hang Your Wash on Someone Else's Line   15

Chapter Three: Dancing in the Hog Trough   35

Chapter Four: Shut the Door! You Weren't Born in a Barn!   60

Chapter Five: Come Hell or High Water   78

Chapter Six: The Porch Light Is Always Burning   100

Chapter Seven: Road Work Ahead   116

About the Author   151

FOREWORD

There isn't one of us who can meander through this world without leaving footprints, good or bad, in and or on the lives of those we bump into. We can only do our utmost to make sure that the imprints we leave behind are stepping-stones that build up, grow, and point others to Christ; not stumbling blocks that may cause others to be stuck in the past and are as worthless as gum on your boot heel!

When I was praying about the foreword for this book, whether to have one or not, I came across a foreword penned by an author's well-known son that was sidesplitting, heart-wrenching, and left a strong and powerful impression on my mind. This encounter of the best kind compelled me to think back upon those women who have radically impacted my life. Whether good or bad, the relationships I have or have had with these ladies have indeed left lasting ripples, indentations, and fingermarks upon my heart, mind, and soul. Six women came to mind; my grandmother, Eula, who raised me; my mother, Wilma, who gave me away; my sister, Peggy, who was oftentimes my bodyguard and best friend; my adulthood best friend, spiritual mama, and mentor, Robin; my daughter, Michelle, someone I can't imagine my life without; and last but not least, my granddaughter, Savannah, my mini-me! Since the first three have now walked into the great over-yonder, I reckon I am privileged to have the eulogy before I kick the bucket and plumb humbled by these beautiful ladies muchly valued and humbling thoughts about the impact my writing and I have had upon their lives. Honest-to-Pete their generous and flattering words, included below, had me blubbing like a baby and grinnin' like a possum eatin' a sweet tater.

My Mommy

I won't lie and say that there isn't a bag of mixed emotions to sort through whenever I hear the words, "I'm writing another book," come out of my mother's lips. You just never know what may end up being shared with the world in her next offering and when you were the type of kid I was, that can be a very scary thing to consider. I'm not saying that my mom just writes about me, but I am saying when you earn the nickname "demon seed" as a child, you may have given her a lot of material to use.

In all seriousness, it's not easy to reflect on the events of your past. It's even harder to share those moments with others, let alone total strangers. It takes a person of great moral fiber and mental fortitude to be able to relive those moments and reflect on the impact that God had at that time, but my mom does just that. In her third book, Friends Don't Let Friends Drive Naked, she takes you on another verbal voyage through the ups and downs of her life in a way that no one else can. The masterful way she details the events of her life leaves you feeling like you were right alongside of her, through the thick and thin. Couple that with her unique tone of voice and use of language that can only be described as "Texanese," and you are left feeling a connection to my mom like you have known her your whole life.

I have been a part of these stories in one way or another my entire life, either by hearing them being told or by being directly involved. It still puts me in awe to be able to sit down and read my mother's version of the events paired with how God moved in them. Her down-home charm, hilarious antics, and soul-shaking revelations will make you bust a gut, grab for the tissues, and have you wondering, "what else could this woman get herself into?"

—Michelle (Daughter & Best friend)

My Gaga

My Gaga has been selfless, kind, and strong. She is a superhero, a mother, a grandmother, a writer, a baker, and a teacher. Most importantly, she is the embodiment of love. From a young age, I was taught that it is not what has happened to you that has defined you, but how you choose to react to those things. My grandmother is the kind of woman who will cradle you while you sob over your own issues even if she's just had knee surgery and can't leave her bed. My grandmother is my rock. She is the epitome of what grace, forgiveness, and hope look like. I was always called my Gaga's "mini-me." It was always such a compliment to think I looked just like her or reminded people of her, but truthfully every part of me has always hoped I would be her "mini-me" because of my heart, my faith, and my strength. I have always wanted to be just like my Gaga. When I first started seeing my grandmother's writing, I wanted to be an author too. I used to write tons of stories. I tried to base them on faith like she would. I tried to articulate the love and goodness that is Jesus. I tried to use southern sayings I had heard her use. I tried to make it so humorous someone would pee from laughing so hard. I realized as I grew older and began to be able to truly understand her writings that it is so much more than a testimony, it is more than thoughts put into profound words. Her writings were her highest form of praise. I used to think she was an actual angel handpicked to come to the earth. I could never fathom how someone could have such a capacity for love or a capacity to treat others with that love. I am forever grateful to have been able to grow up with my eyes set on her and set on Jesus because of her. The impact she has had on my life is immeasurable. She is so much more than just my grandmother and I am so proud and blessed to be able to see her share herself and her talent through her books. The most important thing my grandmother did was teach me about Jesus, show me Jesus in her actions, and help continue to guide me on His path. If it were not for her, I wouldn't have the greatest gift on earth, a relationship with my Savior. I am forever grateful for my Gaga and I hope through her books she can touch your minds, hearts, and souls as deeply as she has nurtured mine.

Gaga, I love you beyond words - you are one of a kind. Thank you for everything you have done and continue to do for me. Pride is not enough of a word to describe how I feel about your accomplishments. You are still and forever my angel, superhero, favorite baker, and Satan's biggest fear.

—Savannah (Granddaughter, Mini-Me)

Miss Kathy

Kathy and I met well over twenty years ago when she walked into the church. I had no idea at the time the special friendship and "Heart connection" that would grow through the years . . . but it did! Our friendship is one of God's sweetest blessings in my life. With Kathy, I can laugh until I cry and cry until I laugh again, sometimes all at the same time! She has been one of my biggest *defenders and encouragers. She has walked with me through some of the happiest times of my life as well as through some of the most challenging and painful. She accepts me as I am, flawed and broken into pieces, and sees the potential and gifts in me even when I can't.*

She is a natural-born teacher and I have had the joy of watching her "fly" as she embraced this gift of hers. I have seen her . . . and the ones she teaches. . . . grow and deepen their walk with Jesus. He is her first passion, and she speaks of Him with sweet abandonment, sharing His love with anyone who will listen! He shines in all she does. Her other passion is her precious family! She loves them with all she has and does! She is a faithful and "full of love" wife, mom, and Gaga!

And then, how she loves the people God has placed in her life! She is there to listen, challenge, and encourage the many who are drawn to her and those she senses need a listening ear.

I know anyone who reads her writings, the lessons she's learned, the wisdom she imparts, the joy she spreads, and the honesty and humor with which she shares, will be blessed beyond what words can measure.

I have been blessed through a friendship for "the ages" by walking some of this journey with her and getting the privilege of calling her friend . . . and family of the heart.

—Robin (Friend, Mentor, Sister from another mother)

I'm beholden to each of these priceless women in my life for their encouraging and generous words, and so very thankful for God's divine intervention that has permitted me to be blessed by their presence and influence in and upon my life.

PREFACE

Good gravy it's been quite a spell since my last book. And if I'm gonna be honest with y'all, I must fess up that I never intended on this book making its' grand entrance into the publishing realm.

But God . . .

Now for those of you who may not have read *Spiritual Laxative for the Constipated Soul* or *You Don't Dig for Water Under the Outhouse*, I must forewarn you that I tend to chase squirrels, fall down rabbit holes, and meander down memory lane while recounting my wild adventures and faith-developing lessons in a foreign language that I so proudly describe as, "Texanese!" Yeehaw!

And honest-to-Pete, how I wrangled with whether to use the title of this book, "Friends Don't Let Friends Drive Naked"! Only because I knew coming up with a concept for a cover that wouldn't send some folks running for higher ground or others getting their undies all wadded in a bunch, was like nailing Jello to a wall!

But God . . .

Any hoot, my aim in writing my books has never been to line my pockets with gold but to spur others on with lofty but bona fide tales of the beautiful and bumpy roads I've traveled in this outrageous and way-too-nonsensical world. I hope that as I expose my unsightly driving skills, heavy-going collisions, out-of-the-blue injuries, staggering road fiascos, and beautiful pearls of wisdom while traveling through this life is that I might be able to transport you, if need be, kicking and screaming, to the throne of a perfect God who I know by up close and personal familiarity loves us faithfully, sacrificially, and way beyond rhyme or our reasoning. Trust me! Better yet, trust Him!

Someone once declared to me, right after I deposited my faith and trust in Christ, that living a life sold-out to Christ would be like a Sunday evening drive! Any hoot, we have a saying in Texas (pardon my Texanese),

"Don't piddle down my back and tell me it is raining!" translated simply means "Don't lie to me!" You just can't spit in my face and call it rain! I just won't sit still for that!

All that to say, I'm just not sure what state of denial or yellow brick road they were skipping down, or the map they were sticking to that gave them that notion! I'm a Texas girl living in a Pennsylvania world, where heavens-to Betsy the state flower should be declared the traffic cone, potholes are so whopping big that they have swimming hours and viewing times; and so plentiful that the state flower grows in them unrestrained, for what seems like an eternity. The road is testing, jarring, unreliable, and treacherous, and fellow travelers can be downright positively unpredictable, road raging, inconsiderate, too big for their britches, exasperating, and from time to time, rest area to rest area, all-out draining.

But God . . .

Because we were born to be wild, life is a highway, a never-ending freeway of love, a long and winding road that if we choose to neglect the directions and trust in the map maker and the map we've been given, can instantaneously turn into the road to nowhere that just might lead us down the "highway to hell." I admit road trips can be exciting but there are times when we think we are the "king of the road," just itching to get our kicks on Route 66, get on the road again, that is any road, even if it is a dead end with no particular place to go. In our haste to drive our life away, satisfy our need for speed, and do it our way, we end up in a roundabout of treacherous curves singing here I go again on my own, where we can't drive 55, running on empty, road-worn and weary, and need to just take it easy. And I reckon if we were honest from the get-go there have been many occasions where we've found ourselves delayed, detoured, or in a traffic jam all because we thought we could control the conditions and the people we encounter on the road when what we needed to be do doing all along was just "let Jesus take the wheel!" I'm preachin' or is that singin' to the choir y'all!

Cross my heart and hope to spit, my unanticipated journey would be so much graver if I was undertaking the driving all by my little lonesome. Trust me! I get sidetracked way too easily, y'all. Indeed, surrendering my life and giving over control of the wheel to my Savior transformed my driving habits and the route I was headed down. Cross my heart and hope to spit, it did not always alter the out-of-my-control road conditions and travelers or pedestrians who I haphazardly collided with, or the unsuspecting passengers who journeyed alongside me on the high-ways and bye-ways of this life.

Now before we commence to begin to get ready to start our engines, I best shed some light on the phrase, "Trust me." I am a practical joker and that is no joke! I love to surprise, prank, and make people giggle till tears are coursing down their legs. When our rugrats (children) were growing up, the rubber snakes, fake spiders, and pranks kept them hopping. In fact, there were so many unruly shenanigans going on in our house that we had to come up with a safe word or else! We had no choice! Trust me! You could be on fire but if you wanted to be taken dead-on seriously, you had best lead with the words, "Trust me!" Who would have thunk it!

In fact, for many practical reasons (insert eye rolling here) there has been a pressing need to share the safe word with my friends. So, to be clear, if I say, "Trust me" it's the same as me saying, "I'm not piddling down your back and telling you it's raining"! Cross my heart and hope to spit! (My safe sentence when trust me isn't enough.) I pinky swear promise! (Just in case the other two don't work!) Oh my! Beating a dead horse doesn't make it taste better. Not that I know! Trust me!

Any hoot, while traveling down this bumpy road with my Lord and Savior, I have undergone so many events that I did not want to endure or that I would not have chosen for my journey. But in my excursions, I have been privy to the fact that God has, can, and will most certainly use all things for His good purpose, that is if I'm willing to let him do the driving.

On this highway of life, I've experienced moments of heavenly bliss, holy laughter, and heart-wrenching despair. I have been broken down alongside the road, my heart hemorrhaging tear upon tear upon tear to the point of it feeling as if it was as empty as a poor man's wallet. I have been run over, cast aside, betrayed, and befriended; loved, and hated; beaten down and built up; a stepping-stone and a stumbling block. But at no point, and in no way, form or fashion have I ever doubted that my

God is a good, good Father and incapable of doing the impossible. Had it not been for His GPS ("God's Protective System"), I'm not so sure I'd be here to give an account of His divine intervention and expert driving know-how.

I have a sweet fondness for the following quote that so expresses the woman of God I hanker to be on this highway of life.

I want to be the kind of woman that when my feet hit the floor in the morning, the devil says, "Oh crap, she's up!"

But too often I must admit I've fallen short of my hankering to be a thorn in the flesh of the father of lies all because I've taken my eyes off my heavenly Father and cozied up too long in the bosom of the world's self-destructing thinking and reckless ways. I reckon you could say that sometimes I have fallen victim to the devil's destructive lies and become more of the poster child for his lie-believing ways than a wound-inflicting pain in his heel—bet you thought I was gonna say *butt*—of the enemy. But my saving grace is, and has always been, the truth of who God is, despite what the world says or what I feel or experience.

Sometimes I just scratch my head and wonder why we sometimes expect life here on earth to be like heaven when we know we are living in a damaged world! It's just the truth, y'all! You can't leisurely travel down this ever-changing road of life and not be distressed by all the brokenness and ruthless driving choices. Because of unforeseen hit-n-runs, drive-bys, and head-on collisions, there are wrecked parts of my heart that God is still in the process of restoring. But trust me, I am pulling out all the stops and am Holy Spirit compelled and determined to be the kind of woman that makes the devil cry in his Wheaties every time he hears my name.

Truth-be-told, I can't even entertain the notion that I was born to fit in! When living like the world will only lead to lane straddling and we all know that crow and corn can't grow in the same field! (You can't serve two masters!) So, I am endeavoring, one day at a time, to stay in His lane, to put a smile on my Father's face and a tear of joy in His eye as I seek to drive through this life in such a way that gives Him all glory, honor, and praise while cruising through this world that most assuredly is not my rest area. Yep, Lord knows there is roadwork ahead and I am a work in progress! And indeed, my loving Father God has His hands full!

As I take a quick glance into the rear-view mirror of my life, I'm so very thankful He can deal with me, even though there have been and will be times when He needs to take me to the woodshed. I'm sure my husband wishes he could! Bless his heart!

As you read through the pages of my life's short journey, in light of the eternal high way, I hope that in my struggles, joys, fears, discouragements, imperfections, poor driving, far-sightedness, near-sightedness, night-blindness, or whatever else may spill onto these pages you will get a glimpse of God's divine help as you experience the strength, hope, love, grace, power, and faithfulness of God that I have become so familiar with in my travels.

1 Samuel 7:12 — *"Then Samuel took a stone and set it up between Mizpah and Shen. He named it Ebenezer, saying, 'Thus far the Lord has helped us.'"*

The prophet Samuel set up a stone after the Lord rerouted the Philistines and gave Israel victory over them. Yes, Israel had to make some directional changes; repentance, seeking the Lord, putting away false gods, and praying. But the stone hailed and honored that sweet conquest! So, whenever the Israelites would pass by the stone, they would bring to mind how the Lord took action on their behalf! I could sit still for that!

But God . . .

The Lord is acting on our behalf and He is faithful, loving, and good all the time!

At the publishing of this book, it has been three long years since my only sister, my younger sister, went home unexpectedly to be with the Lord. On the day of her shocking and hasty departure, I had listened to a song on the radio that I realized she would appreciate, so I texted her the link, knowing it would bring joy and comfort to her weary heart.

My sister had just gone through months of difficult and painful radiation and had been declared cancer free, but she was in a world of suffering and constant pain for which the doctors could not diagnose the source. I thought the song, "Fires" by Jordan St. Cyr would raise her spirits and strengthen her resolve during her time of immense distress. Little did I know that she would never get to hear it!

But God . . .

I now believe that God intended that song for me more than my sweet sister. He knew I would need to be reminded of His sweet all-knowing presence when the dreadful phone call came late that night! I am so thankful for the memories I have with my sweet sister. She was Texas proud, beautiful, and strong! She fought (literally) for me as we traveled together down some of the roughest and most strenuous roads when we were only teenagers out on our very own. We tended to and protected one another when no one else seemed to take any notice of our existence or situation. We were not brought up in the same household, but our hearts could not be separated by distance. I miss our talks, mes-saging, gif wars, her strength and laughter. I miss her voice. Most of all, I miss the comfort of knowing that even though miles separated us we were both looking up at the same sky. Although hers was bigger, since it is a "Texas" sky y'all! My heart can scarcely take it all in and my eyes leak when I think upon it!

That night when I got the call, all I could do was fall to my knees and scream, "Not Peggy!" I then locked myself away in the bathroom, dropped to the floor, and wept as I listened to the song I had sent her that morning. (God and I have our best encounters on the bathroom floor!) I played the song over and over, and over again. And I sobbed till my eye sockets were dryer than Texas dirt. The words still manage to make me smile and cry all at the same time.

So, long before I realized I would have a need; the need to be carried, encouraged, and reminded of His presence traveling with me through the fire and valley of my intense grief; to be comforted and held, God prepared and lit the way through the shadow of death. He so tenderly reminded me too that He is faithful and keeps His promises. And that one day because of His faithfulness and love. . . . I will see my sister again!

But God . . .

"My flesh and my heart may fail, 'But God . . .' is the strength of my heart and my portion forever." (Psalm 73:26)

Indeed, the road is bone-weary long, travelers unreliable, road condi-tions terrible, visibility sometimes low or not all, but God . . . can take a hopeless situation, the unknown road, the ashes of our past, our poor driving decisions, the careless driving of others and transform them into sacred and fruitful stepping-stones! Stones of Remembrance of the power of God to do what man deems impossible! Ashes aren't the end of my story, and they don't have to be yours.

As you travel alongside me, over the hills and valleys and through the remnants of my wild unpredictable journey, who knows what or who you may encounter! All I am sure of is this: we do not have to do it on our own! We do not have to travel alone and unprepared! Friends don't let friends drive naked! It's time to hit the road, Jack!

CHAPTER ONE

ALL HAT NO CATTLE

I must say that for as long as I have permitted my dear children to breathe, they have derived quite a bit of amusement in my—for lack of a better word—ignorance. Now, mind you, it wasn't till a good number of years back that I had the slightest inkling of understanding what the seemingly insulting word even meant. Trust me! In fact, several years back I sat in my store with a sweet girl from my church just chewing the fat when our conversation turned toward my innocence and how stupid I felt I was. I can still hear her plainspoken words slapping me across the face, "Miss Kathy, you aren't stupid, you're just ignorant!"

Honest-to-Pete I was so shell-shocked by her gumption and forth-rightness that I reckon you could have slapped me into next Tuesday with a feather! No one had ever called me ignorant before—well, at least to my face. Stupid, yes! But ignorant, never! Of course, after researching the definition of the misleading word, I understood exactly what the sweet, unashamed, and fearlessly honest young lady was trying to get across to me.

Faster than a sneeze through a screen door, ignorance became my newfangled word for the day. Truth-be-told, I can bear witness to the fact that it has often been out of ignorance that I have acted a might stupidly. You can take that to the bank, but you may not be able to cash it! Hoot there it is! In Texas, we would just say, "Yep, she just fell off the turnip truck!"

I can't begin to tally up the countless number of times my fearless—or should I say "ignorant"—kids who had me convinced of something that wasn't true at all, have exclaimed, without any thought for their safety, and with way too much laughter for their own good, "Oh Mom, you're so gullible!" (Yes, another word I had to look up!)

My mama and my grandmother loved to threaten us with, "I brought you into this world and I can take you out!"

Good golly Miss Molly, how I wish I'd had the forethought to record my rugrats' birthing! Then gullible ol' me could have watched their dumbfounded faces as I played back the recording of their entrance into this world in reverse and as proof that I indeed brought them into this world and that I most certainly had the means and wherewithal to take them out!

In hindsight, it would have been funny as all get-out but also pretty stupid on my part, because those saplings of mine weren't as gullible as their mama. In this case, I guess you could say the apple fell far from the tree. Ain't that a hoot!

I reckon it's a fact that stupid is as stupid does and that my actions at one time or another might have had some onlookers scratching their heads and questioning if I had put my brain in my back pocket and sat on it. My grandmother used to say, "If ignorance (there's that word again) were bliss, Katherine Mae, then you would be in heaven!" (I always knew I was in trouble when she used my full first and middle name.)

I guess it is a cold hard fact that I do tend to have my head stuck high up in the clouds. Hoot, there it is!

Cross my heart and hope to spit, it's the God's honest truth that I just don't always get people's jokes or innuendoes; I'm a might more inclined than some to take most people at face value. I must confess that my ignorance has from time to time led to some mighty impressive and entertaining drama, not to mention tears-running-down-the-legs laughter for quite a few bystanders or victims. So, I reckon it ain't all bad now, is it? If you are shaking your head and grinning right now, that's okay! As my grandmother would often say, "Shake it, don't break it! It took your mama nine months to make it!"

Some years back I launched my own quilt and country store. I took great pleasure in the time spent at my store, and it was there that I got to become acquainted with so many awe-inspiring ladies as well as share my sweet Jesus with several. Woo Hoo! Well, don't you know, one sweltering summer day, I just happened to gaze out my store window, which looked onto the main road, to see rambling down the street a man who looked a whole lot like Jesus lugging a large wooden white cross the size of the one our Savior was executed on. I'm serious as the business end of a .45! Now may I ask you, who wouldn't, in their right or left mind, if they had a chance, want to have a sit-down with someone who gave the impression he was living like Jesus! Now mind you, I may be gullible, even stupid, but what I ain't is born yesterday! I knew the dark long-haired, bearded, sandal-clad, white-robed man wasn't the genuine Jesus, but boy oh boy, did he look and dress exactly like what most of us would envision our Jesus to be. So, I did what any godly woman hell-bent on having a dialogue with Jesus would do. I snatched an icy-cold bottle of water from the store fridge, hung up the closed sign on the storefront door, and leapt into my trusty van to chase after the retreating figure.

As I pulled over to the side of the road, immediately behind his destination-determined figure, I began to get a tad bit uneasy. I mean this guy was literally taking up his cross daily! What would I, could I, or should I say to him? I warily walked up behind the Jesus look-alike and yelled over the irritatingly loud noise of the passing traffic, "Jesus!"

In my defense, what else could I call the man? It's too late for suggestions so please don't bother. Well, don't you know, when the Jesus look-alike spun around and looked at me didn't I get so nervous that I almost choked on my tongue! Honest-to-Pete, anyone who knows me will testify and pinky swear to the fact that I'm not ordinarily the silent type, but I ain't whistling dixie when I say that there was something about standing eye to eye with a living, breathing, walking look-a-like of Jesus that made my mouth feel like I'd been sucking on lemons for a month.

I quickly offered the Jesus look-alike the bottle of cold, refreshing water and waited long-sufferingly as he took a long drink. Can I just say that in that eternal-now moment, I was plumb tickled pink inside! I kid you not! All I could think about while the Jesus look-alike was gulping down his water was the Samaritan woman at the well.

"Oh yeah, oh yeah, I'm giving Jesus water! Who is the good girl now Lord!"

Well, reality sunk in like a pig in fresh mud as I snapped out of my daydream only to discover that the Jesus-double had not only put his water bottle away but had plucked up his homemade cross and strode away, leaving me standing there dazed and confused with not even a thank you, God bless you my child, go and sin no more, or a see you on the other side! I just couldn't conceive in my ignorant, gullible great brain of my Jesus doing such an insensitive and unloving thing!

So, I pursued him! Jesus is not the only one who can be relentless, y'all! When the Jesus look-alike grasped the full reality of his dire situation; that I was not going to be shaken off that effortlessly, he came to a sudden dead stop at the side of the busy road, deposited his well-traveled cross on the ground, and quickly spun around to give me his full undivided attention (gulp). And our conversation went something like this . . .

ME, the Jesus fan: *Hi! Uh, I really don't know what to call you, but I saw you walking down the street, carrying the cross and I just had to come and talk to you.*

Anyone who knows me would state under oath to the fact that at that second, I was giddier than an outhouse fly! Oh, happy day!

Not THE Jesus: *(insert cricket sound)*

ME, the Jesus fan: (Feeling a tad bit uncomfortable) *Uh, I just really wanted to know why you are doing what you are doing? You know carrying the cross all over the United States while dressed like Jesus!*

I was sure that his response would grow me by leaps and bounds!

Not THE Jesus: *"I'm writing a book!"*

It was not the answer I was looking for y'all, but I was more than happy to give him some slack since it was a scorching clammy day, and the rough wooden cross looked mighty weighty, and he did have an uncanny likeness to the Jesus in my grandmother's light-up velvet paintings.

ME, the Jesus fan: *Wow! So, what are you writing a book about?*

I knew an eye-opening, heart-inspiring, faith-building answer was headed in my direction!

Not THE Jesus: *"I'm writing about all the places I've traveled to."*

Really?! This guy is traveling all over the USA, carrying a cross while dressed like Jesus, and all he is writing about is the places he has visited. Disappointment hit me like a two-by-four! And needless to say, I was feeling a might cross! (Punny happens!)

ME, the Jesus fan: *Oh! Well okay, you have a blessed day!*

Yes, I was speechless. Trust me, that doesn't happen often!

Not THE Jesus: *"Can I ask you a question?"*

Woo hoo! At last! I was ready for a Sermon on the Mount message!

ME, the Jesus fan: *Fire away!*

My hopes rose to an all-time high! I had God-bumps on top of my freckles! I kid you not!

Not THE Jesus: *"Where is the nearest motel?"*

I felt like all the oxygen had just been sucked out of the atmosphere as a whole mess of disappointment settled upon my chest! That was not the question I anticipated nor longed for!

I just assumed our conversation would be more Jesus-like, you know!

Not THE Jesus: *"Can you give me a lift? I'm pretty sure my cross will fit in your van."* (as he gave my van a thorough once over by walking to back, opening the van doors, and checking the cargo area)

I don't know why, but his question startled the fearless Texan blood plumb right out of me! God-bumps were swapped with goosebumps as I heard the Psycho sound effects hammering in my heart and images of the shower scene murder from the Bate's motel frolicked in my startled brain.

ME, the Jesus fan: (Oozing sincerity and shaking in my blinged-out flip-flops) *I'm sorry but my husband, who is a police officer, has always instructed me that I shouldn't pick up strangers because it's too dangerous! I'm sure you understand!*

Not THE Jesus: (Shaking head side to side in obvious disagreement.)

ME, the Jesus fan: *Uh, I realize that you look like Jesus, uh, and that you're dressed like Jesus and all, and that you are hauling that life-size cross all over the countryside, but I'm sure you can grasp why I just can't do it! I'm so sorry!*

God's word was sprinting through my brain, prompting and convicting me to remember that whatever you do for the least of these you do for Him! If this was a test then I was flunking, big time!

Not THE Jesus: (angry) *"Well, you should care more about what God says than your husband!"*

I was not prepared for his brashness or his anger!

Right then and there I recalled Jesus wise words when He was being tempted by Satan for forty days in the wilderness; that *"man does not live my bread alone but by every word from the mouth of God"* and I did what any Godly woman would do and called upon scripture to help me out from between a rock and a hard place!

ME, the Jesus fan: (Stomping my feet) *Well, I do care what God wants and I just think that God would want me to "submit to my husband!"*

Yes, I did it! I admit I have a thinking problem! And yes, before my brain could engage, I pulled a rabbit out of my hat and used the whole *"wives submit to your husband"* scripture as a reason to dodge lending a hand to an irritated and not so nice Jesus look-alike.

Who would have thunk it?

Not THE Jesus: (Really angry) *"You obviously don't know or love God! If you did you would take me to the motel! I will pray for your salvation!"*

I was flabbergasted, dumbfounded, and wounded beyond words as the Jesus look-alike, but not my Jesus, huffily picked up his big ol' cross, purposely turned his not so holy back on me, and heatedly stormed away. I can still hear the not so divine pitter-patter of his flip-flops hitting the hot pavement!

So, I rushed back to my car, head hanging down in shame as tears gushed from my eyes.

As I sat there in my car and gawked at the retreating back of the not-so-nice Jesus look-alike inch further and further away into the distant Texas sun, I frantically tried to phone a friend. I just needed to hear somebody, anybody, tell me what I should do next! But as hard as I tried, I could not get hold of one soul! So, I just sat there in my car sobbing like I'd been chewed up, spit out, and stepped on!

After some serious soul searching and a few pity-party moments I revved up my non-cross carrying van and drove up behind the withdrawing figure of the not-so-nice Jesus look-alike. With the faith of Daniel in the lion's den, I leapt out of my vehicle and with the courage of David facing Goliath, hollered over the noisy traffic the only profound truth that I knew to set this Jesus look-alike straight, "You know what! I do love God and I AM saved! So there!" (That's telling him!)

Not being one to stand around to get whooped like a red-headed stepchild, I ran as fast as I could to the security of my van, locked all the doors, and sped away, disappointed, disillusioned, and saddened. Call me stupid, naïve, gullible, or ignorant, if you will, but I just supposed he would act like Jesus!

I must say that I do not deem myself to be quite as gullible or ignorant as I used to be. That proclamation alone makes me want to shed tears in my Cheerios for more excuses than I can shake a stick at. If I'm going to expose my soul to you, then I must let you know that this is not the most comfortable chapter for me to write. Even though I do find humor in things, I also can't help but feel woeful when I recognize that we exist in a world that is as baffled as a goat on Astroturf. Truth is based on feelings, experiences, circumstances, and the world's opinions more than the faithfulness, steadfastness, and trustworthiness of our heavenly Father and His word.

I guess that is why trust, more often than not, has to be deserved and discernment is a must if you want to walk away with all your fingers and toes and not end up as buzzard bait!

I disclosed in the beginning of this book that a much-used phrase around our house was and still is "Trust Me." I used to find it funny and harmless when I had to use it to ensure that someone knew what I was communicating to them was the truth, the whole truth, and nothing but the truth. But now when I think on it my heart frowns and groans a bit. I ache for my children and grandchildren to trust me, not because I use the safe-word or a magical phrase, but because I am deemed trustworthy. Now I know some of my stories may need to end with "Trust Me" because they can seem wilder than an acre of snakes. But if you haven't witnessed it yet, this world is nuttier than a five-pound fruitcake and that can be just about as depressing as a two-car funeral. Trust me, I know!

Truth-be-told, I aspire to be the sort of woman that when I say a hen dips snuff, you can peek under its wing and find the snuff can. Truth is crucial, but where we get it from is just as important. There is an exceptionally good reason as to why you don't drink the water under an outhouse. The water not only reeks to high heaven but is contaminated, can make you green around the gills, give you the runs, and perhaps even send you to meet your maker. A deficiency or lack of truth, getting it from a resource other than the Word of God can lead to truth decay, spiritual anorexia, constipation of thought, diarrhea of mouth, and all-out heart failure! In due course, you just might get so ill that you have to get better just to die! I don't know about you, but I'd just as soon bite a bug than to live my life separated from the truth of my Abba Daddy!

I'm not piddling down your back when I testify to the fact that I have fallen victim to truth decay that had a profound impact on me. I was raised up by my grandmother, who I choose to believe, come hell or high water, loved me but just did not know in what manner or by what means how to love. Her relentless verbal and ever-so-often physical assaults were not only physically and emotionally draining but destructive to my way of thinking. My grandfather, whom I called Papa, was the blockade between my grandmother and me, and oftentimes the stunt double for her verbal and physical lashing outs, which stopped when he died from a sudden heart attack in his sleep when I was nine.

After my grandfather's passing away, my grandmother's anger intensified more than my little girl's heart thought possible. Her demeanor became darker than the devil's riding boots! And if that wasn't enough, her degrading words and wounding actions increased and became crueler as I moved into my adolescent years. Truth-be-told, cuddling with a rose bush would have been much more comforting and a lot less painful than having to hear her shriek the repulsive and spiteful insults that she spewed. Not to mention her threatening ways of waving in the air and making very effective disciplinary use of whatever tool she held in her hands at the time. Running, ducking, and crying were not options if I didn't want to be disciplined much worse later on.

So, all that to say, I grew up accepting the lies she vomited out in her fury and fear as truth. I understood and felt that I was not worth spit! I was certain that I was, as she had hollered time and time again, worthless rubbish, unwanted, and broken goods that no one in their right mind or left for that matter, should, could, or would possibly love. The life-long mistreatment I had become accustomed to came to a head at about age fourteen, nearly fifteen, when I arrived home late from school one day because the bus was running behind schedule. My grandmother went on a rampage and began to point the finger at me for being tardy for unspeakable motives that I can't even begin to spill onto these pages. To this very day, her cruel, groundless, and uncalled-for words still cause the bile to rise in the pit of my stomach when I ponder it. Yet again, the name-calling gushed forth from her corrupt mind, and no matter how much I adamantly denied her accusations or blubbered, she was firmly set in her beliefs and relentless with her malicious words.

I truly don't know if I ran away that day out of anger, hurt, fear for my life, or just because my heart couldn't take it anymore, but that's exactly what I did; I ran. With no place to go, I wandered our small town, going from one home to another for a while until I finally ended up bunking with my sister who was a year younger than me and struggling to survive out in the world all by her lonesome.

So, there I was, at the ripe old age of sixteen, with seventeen ready and looming around the corner, bunking with my sweet sister in a small apartment in a remote area situated on the outskirts of town. It was tough going and even with the two of us girls straining daily to meet our needs to just survive we were so broke that we couldn't even afford a tumbleweed for a pet. After a rough couple of months trying to make ends meet and barely accomplishing that, my sister relocated to her boyfriend's apartment leaving me to my own devices.

On my own now, I could not manage to pay for electricity, but I was happy that I had cold running water, a pot to pee in and a window to throw it out of, a roof over my head, food occasionally, and a bed to rest my head on. But most of all, I had peace!

For a brief time, I labored as a teletype operator for the Abilene Reporter News even though it was 3-4 hours walking distance, depending on the weather and if I was wearing a dress and clogs. Walking to and from work was downright wearying and sometimes painful. Ouch! My work shift was 3 pm-11 pm, so walking home late at night and into the early morning hours was almost certainly not the sensible thing to do, and it was definitely the most unnerving part of my nightly hike home. I can chuckle now, and you are welcome to join in, as I can still visualize myself at 1 am walking down the last lonely stretch of road to my humble abode, afraid of what wicked-minded person might be out at that time of night in search of his prey, ducking in and out of the bushes to hide from passing vehicles. This was me, what can I say!

Any hoot, one day I got wind of a job as a housekeeper at a motel within walking distance of my apartment. No more daily clog hiking and bush ducking for me! Yippee! So, I applied for the job and was pleasantly surprised that the owners were exceedingly kind, welcoming, and extremely grateful to have me. A month or two into my new job I learned that the couple who ran the motel where I worked were Christians when they invited me to their church. Even though I was at the ripe old age of seventeen I had never been to church and had no clue exactly what went on in one. As a young child, my grandmother had insisted and required that I commit to memory the 23rd Psalm as well as recite it to her daily, although I had no inkling as to what it was all about. My grandmother also had beautiful lit-up paintings of Jesus scattered throughout the house and even a whole bathtub full of Bibles to boot. But I reckon the closest those Bibles ever came to getting read was when I fell into a sticker patch, and she had to unload the bathtub so I could take a good long soak.

I wish I could perfectly describe to you the feeling I had on my first visit to a real bona fide church and the profound impact it had on me (Insert angel choir here).

The big white church was massive, immaculate, and jam-packed with so many impeccably dressed people. I pinky swear to the fact that I was almost certain that most of the people attending were proudly parading the very same Bible my grandmother had kept stashed away in her bathtub. The pastor was inviting, the people friendly, and for the first time in a long, long time I felt safe and welcomed. Even though my simple clothes didn't seem to be quite up to par with the fine threads those attending donned, the church-going folk appeared to take no never-mind to my less-than-pristine appearance and came across as genuinely loving and kind as they went out of their way to introduce themselves to the new kid in church. I felt like the couple I worked for had made it their mission to take me under their wing and it was nice to get a glimpse and feel for what being part of a genuine family might really be like.

The pastor, who I promptly put on a pedestal, began his sermon and I was reeled in, hook, line, and sinker by the life-saving message he delivered. It was the first time I had been made aware of the truth of Jesus Christ and what He had done for me. It blew my mind into the next galaxy! I just couldn't wrap my heart or mind around what I was hearing, nor fathom the manner of sacrificial love that Jesus, the Son of God, had for me, a total stranger, that would lead Him to choose to die a horrific death on the cross. The truth sent my heart rocking and swaying!

For the first time in a long time, I became acutely aware that I was not alone; I was loved, and I had a purpose! There was hope! I had hope! The shackle-releasing thought that even though my mama didn't want me, there was this great big ever-loving, almighty, merciful, holy, faithful God who held His arms wide open, even to the cross and was bidding me to be His daughter made me want to get up and dance. So yes ma'am and yes sir! I held back the need I felt to run and walked the spotless church aisle, straight up to the pastor that day and I told Jesus I wanted to be His! Woo Hoo!

A month or two down the yellow-brick road of my new journey as a Christian, the pastor began his new series on the end times. Well, shut my mouth wide open! I discovered that not only did my Jesus love me but that indeed He was coming back to get those who are His. He was coming back to get me! Woo Hoo! When the pastor matter-of-factly declared the date of Jesus' magnificent return, my heart just about leapt out of my chest. I was so excited and motivated that I could spit! I was on a mission now!

I was compelled and propelled by the news that I had only one month to inform everyone in my circle of life that my Jesus was coming to get me and take me home with Him and that it wasn't too late for them to go home too. I went to pay a visit to my boyfriend in the county jail (we won't go there now) and informed him that I couldn't see him anymore cause Jesus was coming back to get me and take me home. Once he was able to slap the look of complete shock off his face and hitch his jaw back up off the floor, he about busted a gut laughing at me. Truth-be-told, I ran away from the county jail that day bawling because he didn't believe me or accept the truth about my Jesus.

And so, the long-awaited and much anticipated day arrived for my Jesus to come and get me. Woo Hoo! I was happier than a hog in mud. Truth-be-told, I really didn't know what to expect! Would He ring the doorbell? Would He just appear before my eyes? What should I wear?

Honest-to-Pete, I most assuredly could see no reason to go to work, so I called up the motel and made it known that I wasn't coming in to work that day. I must admit I was a might surprised to learn that the couple who had taken me to church had even bothered to go to work that day! But I reckoned He IS Jesus, and He would know where to find them! (giggle) As for me, I wasn't moving a muscle and taking no chances, just in case!

Well, I mustered up what meager clothing I possessed and packed it away in a small bag, planted myself in the middle of my empty living room, and waited for my Jesus to come for me. I waited . . . And I waited! Late into the evening I waited!

He never showed!

My very first thought . . . God didn't want me and that all the hurtful and cruel things my grandmother had said were indeed true. That yes indeedy, I was so damaged, so un-loveable that even Jesus didn't want to take me home with Him. I fell asleep in the early morning hours of the next day with that thought weighing heavy on my broken heart!

The next day, grief-stricken and done with it all, I went to garner my final pay from the motel only to discover that the couple who had encouraged me to go to church had also been left behind. Ain't that a hoot! I could only conclude Jesus didn't want them either!

That following Sunday, as I passed the stately church, the cheese fell off my cracker, when I beheld all the bible-toting, well-dressed people spilling out of the church smiling and carrying on like the disappointment of the week before made no never-mind to them.

My second thought . . . Christians are not trustworthy. They indeed are no different than this broken world or those that had unleashed pain in my life. So, from that point forward I resolved in my ignorant and gullible heart that I would not tell my children about God or Jesus. I would let them figure out the truth on their own. And it goes without saying, but I will, that I kept away from anyone who said they were a Christian or who showed up at my door to speak to me about Jesus. It sounded like the right thing to do at the time and so that is just what I did.

But God . . .

Proverbs 14:12-13 — *"There is a way that seems right to a man, but its end is the way of death."*

I was seventeen at the time and it wasn't until 20 years later that I ventured into another church. Another story for another day! Cross my heart and hope to spit! Oh, if I'd only known then what I know now.

The two biggest regrets I have in my life:

1. I believed the lie, didn't search for the truth, and walked away that day from the greatest love of all and the only one who could and would redeem my life from the pit.
2. I, the one that should be a picture of Christ and tell my children the truth about Jesus' sacrificial love, chose to let them be crammed full of the lies of this world instead of being the one who told them the truth.

1 Peter 5:8 Amplified Bible (AMP) — *"Be sober [well balanced and self-disciplined], be alert and cautious at all times. That enemy of yours, the devil, prowls around like a roaring lion [fiercely hungry], seeking someone to devour."*

God, forgive us when sometimes we are one of Satan's most effective and destructive weapons!

WARNING: *If we don't get in the Word of God, we may one day find ourselves suffering from a severe case of truth decay. Ignorance of the word of God is not bliss!*

If we don't get the word of God in us, then we may wake up one day only to discover that we are "All Hat and No Cattle." (All talk and no walk)

And if you think ignoring these warnings is harmless and will affect only you, then have I got a story for you. Trust me! It makes my heart bleed tears when I think about it!

Ephesians 6:10-17 AMP — *"In conclusion, be strong in the Lord [draw your strength from Him and be empowered through your union with Him] and in the power of His [boundless] might. Put on the full armor of God [for His precepts are like the splendid armor of a heavily armed soldier], so that you may be able to [successfully] stand up against all the schemes and the strategies and the deceits of the devil. For our struggle is not against* *flesh and blood [contending only with physical opponents], but against the rulers, against the powers, against the world forces of this [present] darkness, against the spiritual forces of wickedness in the heavenly (supernatural) places. Therefore, put on the complete armor of God, so that you will be able to [successfully] resist and stand your ground in the evil day [of danger], and having done everything [that the crisis demands], to stand firm [in your place, fully prepared, immovable, victorious]. So stand firm and hold your ground, HAVING TIGHTENED THE WIDE BAND OF TRUTH (personal integrity, moral courage) AROUND YOUR WAIST and HAVING PUT ON THE BREASTPLATE OF RIGHTEOUSNESS (an upright heart), and having strapped on YOUR FEET THE GOSPEL OF PEACE IN PREPARATION [to face the enemy with firm-footed stability and the readiness produced by the good news]. Above all, lift up the [protective] shield of faith with which you can extinguish all the flaming arrows of the evil one. And take THE HELMET OF SALVATION, and the sword of the Spirit, which is the Word of God."*

Just Sayin'!

I am not condemning going to church. We need to be in fellowship with the body of Christ. I know that to be true. I am also aware that there is not one perfect person in the body of Christ. But as Christians, we cannot place blame on others for our lack of growth or ignorance of the truth. As Christians, we also have a responsibility, each and every one of us, to rightly divide His truth as well as to be a picture of Christ to others. I hope that I painted a picture of the importance of the truth as well as the devastation we unleash on ourselves and others when we are ignorant of God's word or live apart from His truth.

CHAPTER TWO

DON'T HANG YOUR WASH ON SOMEONE ELSE'S LINE

I know you just might be gawking at the title of this chapter, scratching your head, and questioning where I might be going. Well, hang onto your britches, put your hair net on, and batten down the hatches because as sure as I'm sitting here, I have been known to be guilty of speaking ten words a second with a good chance of gusts up to fifty. I wish this was not a topic that we need to thrash out, but I fear that if we continue to sweep it under the rug it will only lead to a heaping speed bump that more unsuspecting and ignorant victims will stumble and trip over. Now you may be tempted to jump track and move on as you read this chapter, cross my heart and hope to spit, because this is going to be one heck of a ride! So please hang on till the end and don't give up!

I believe one of the biggest problems we may have in our journey with God is the tendency or the temptation to sometimes dib and dab where we do not belong. To travel down roads God has put a big "Do Not Enter" sign across. We look for truth, love, and acceptance in all the wrong places. We expect others to have it all together, especially in the church, and all because we think we do! And when others don't live up to our expectations some of us have been known to stomp our feet, shake our fists, yell, and curse, surprisingly not at the one trespassing God's boundaries, but at our Abba Daddy!

Proverbs 19:3 NIV — *"A person's own folly leads to their ruin, yet their heart rages against the LORD."*

Honestly, you would like to think that of all the joints in all the towns in all the world where you should be able to locate truth, love, and hope it most assuredly would be the church, which is under the banner of Jesus Christ. Y'all, somewhere, somehow down the road we have detoured and fashioned the opinion that every person who attends the church (the physical structure) is also part of the body of Christ (those who have believed and trusted in Christ's atoning work for salvation). Well, I think I'm gonna have to throw down the flag and scream foul on that judgment!

As the saying goes, "If you put a cat in an oven, it doesn't make a biscuit." Truth-be-told, if you deposit a person in a church, it doesn't make them a Christian! Heavens-to-Betsy, we live in a sinful, broken world where unpleasant people happen, sin continues to run rampant, cruel storms rain on our parade, and the truth is a passing fancy based more on what feels good and makes us happy instead of the loving, life-saving protective fencing of God's word. Honest-to-Pete, I reckon a good many of our aches and pains can be accredited to some close encounter of the worst kind with an individual who has a big ol' gaping hole in their fence, no fence at all, or a degree in fence jumping 101.

I'd even go out on a limb, and I'm scared of heights, to be so bold as to say that when those of us who bear the name Christian, have messed up royally and broken our Father's ever-loving heart, it has been because we too took a leisurely drive on the wild, dark, forbidden side by crossing over through a man-made opening in God's protective fence. We let our feelings boss our faith when our faith should be bossing our feelings. Gosh, I have seen some folks even go so far as to tear the fence down or climb right over it. And don't even get me started with the whole fence-straddling excuse! Cottoning to that excuse is like nailing Jell-O to the wall! Truth-be-told, fence-straddling has been known to trigger chafed sensitive thighs that in due time, if left unattended, could result in a very agonizing limp or crawl.

I hark back to a time when as teenagers, my sister and I would wander and explore the grand Texas countryside. Frankly, it's downright distressing when I mull over all the strange and precarious places we stumbled upon late at night. I hate to admit it, but there were many times when we clambered over some mighty tall barbed-wire fences, all the while turning a blind eye to the very noticeable warning signs posted, cautioning us not to trespass. I won't even take the risk of talking about our late-night missile silo excursion. Shhhh! It's a secret!

I'll plead guilty to the fact that there were a few times in my young life when I came home with ripped pants, cuts, bruises, and a sore bleeding behind due to the sheer fact that I elected not to use the big brain God gave me by talking myself into thinking the barbed wire at the top of the fence was only a visual deterrent that truly couldn't do any damage. I reckon we thought we were fearless and adventurous, but as I look back in the rearview mirror, I can honestly say we were just plumb reckless and stupid. Shucks, we can't even plead ignorance because we would read the warning signs and choose to blatantly ignore them. I'm pretty sure most of us who have vaulted over the fence of God's protective will can identify and testify, Knowledge is knowing a tomato is a fruit. Wisdom is not putting a tomato in a fruit salad! But as Forest Gump said, "Stupid is as stupid does." "And that's all I have to say about that!"

That being said, I just can't cotton to nor do I wholly grasp the thinking process of an individual who will choose to unashamedly leap, straddle, or tear down the protective fence, and then when they come face to face, nose to nose, toe to toe with the consequences of their choices on the not-so-green grass side of the fence, pitch a hissy fit and stomp away mad, not at themselves, but at God! It makes me crazier than a wet hen when we fence jump and then blame God for our choice to drop the gun and hug the grizzly. And it makes me even crazier, if that is possible, when we blame God for other folks' fence-hopping. Just being real, y'all!

James 1:13-15 New Living Translation (NLT) — *"And remember, when you are being tempted, do not say, 'God is tempting me.' God is never tempted to do wrong, and he never tempts anyone else. Temptation comes from our own desires, which entice us and drag us away. These desires give birth to sinful actions. And when sin is allowed to grow, it gives birth to death."*

There is a goal for the protective fence of God's will, and it is not to keep us in but to safeguard us from the strange, dangerous outcomes lurking on the other side that will most assuredly steal our joy, kill our relationships, and if given the opportunity, destroy us spiritually, emotionally, and possibly physically. If we think our rebellious choices don't or won't have an impact on anyone but ourselves then you can take it to the bank when I say that it won't be long before one and all within the range of our blasting zone will be eating sorrow by the spoonful.

I've seen firsthand the hazardous fallout, wounding repercussions, and grim consequences of my rebellious fence-straddling decisions breed like maggots in the lives of those around me. It's true that as Christians we are forgiven, thank you Lord, but His forgiveness does not mean that all the consequences of our fence-jumping are erased. As Christians, the called-out ones, His grace does not hand us a hall pass to live out our lives choosing to repeatedly straddle or hop the fence of God's protective will. If we believe that it does, then we just might not appreciate nor grasp the fullness, beauty, and power of God's grace. And that's all I have to say about that!

I can't help but be troubled and riled when I am privy to others struggling with the existence and character of God, all because someone in their circle of influence, who professes to love God and follow Jesus, has not only jumped the fence, pitched a tent and settled in for the winter on the other side of God's protective will, but has also felt they have every right to grab the fence post, barbed wire and all, and bash their unsuspecting victim on the head with it. All the while leaving the target of their log-in-eye malady, running away as fast as their feet will carry them with the mistaken or false conclusion that all those that identify as Christians are hypocrites and even worse, that God must not exist because they do not see the effect of a life transformed by the power of God!

Excuse me while I saddle up this pony and ride for a spell. I just got to say right here and now, that dog won't and don't hunt! I just am not certain that a Christian can be a hypocrite! Wait for it! I just wrestle with the notion that a person who sincerely places their life into the nail-pierced hands of Jesus, trusting Him with all their oomph can be a hypocrite, a pretender, or a fraud! Don't give up on me, hang onto your saddle horn! Trust me, this is not the gospel according to Kathy so please bear with me as we look at the sobering words Jesus had to say about the hypocritical Scribes and the Pharisees.

Matthew 23:10-31 — *"Then Jesus said to the crowds and to his disciples, The teachers of religious law and the Pharisees are the official interpreters of the law of Moses.* **So, practice and obey whatever they tell you, but don't follow their example. For they don't practice what they teach. They**

crush people with agonizing religious burdens and never lift a finger to ease the weight.

"Everything they do is for show. On their arms they wear extra wide prayer boxes with Scripture verses inside, and they wear robes with extra-long tassels. And they love to sit at the head table at banquets and in the seats of honor in the synagogues. They love to receive respectful greetings as they walk" in the marketplaces, and to be called 'Rabbi.'

I used the NLT translation here, but in some other translations it will say, "Woe to you!" In this translation, it says, "What sorrow awaits you!" Jesus used "Woe" in these scriptures seven times! Oh no! This is serious stuff so pin your ears back, listen up!

*"**What sorrow awaits you (Woe to you!)** teachers of religious law and you Pharisees. **Hypocrites! For you shut the door of the Kingdom of Heaven in people's faces. You won't go in yourselves, and you don't let others enter either.***

*"What sorrow awaits you (Woe to you) teachers of religious law and you Pharisees. **Hypocrites! For you cross land and sea to make one convert, and then you turn that person into twice the child of hell you yourselves are! (Yikes)***

*"Blind guides! What sorrow awaits you (Woe to you) For you say that it means nothing to swear 'by God's Temple,' but that it is binding to swear 'by the gold in the Temple.' **Blind fools!** Which is more important— the gold or the Temple that makes the gold sacred? And you say that to swear 'by the altar' is not binding, but to swear 'by the gifts on the altar' is binding. How blind! For which is more important—the gift on the altar or the altar that makes the gift sacred? When you swear 'by the altar,' you are swearing by it and by everything on it. And when you swear 'by the Temple,' you are swearing by it and by God, who lives in it. And when you swear 'by heaven,' you are swearing by the throne of God and by God, who sits on the throne."*

*"**What sorrow awaits you (Woe to you)** teachers of religious law and you Pharisees. **Hypocrites!** For you are careful to tithe even the tiniest income from your herb gardens, but **you ignore the more important aspects of the law—justice, mercy, and faith.** You should tithe, yes, but do not neglect*

the more important things. **Blind guides! You strain your water so you won't accidentally swallow a gnat, but you swallow a camel!**

"What sorrow awaits you (Oh no!) teachers of religious law and you Pharisees. **Hypocrites! For you are so careful to clean the outside of the cup and the dish, but inside you are filthy—full of greed and self-indulgence!** *You blind Pharisee! First wash the inside of the cup and the dish, and then the outside will become clean, too.*

"What sorrow awaits you (Oh no!) teachers of religious law and you Pharisees. **Hypocrites!** *For you are like* **whitewashed tombs—beautiful on the outside but filled on the inside with dead people's bones and all sorts of impurity. Outwardly you look like righteous people, but inwardly your hearts are filled with hypocrisy and lawlessness.**

"What sorrow awaits you (Oh no!) teachers of religious law and you Pharisees. **Hypocrites!** *For you build tombs for the prophets your ancestors killed, and you decorate the monuments of the godly people your ancestors destroyed. Then you say, 'If we had lived in the days of our ancestors, we would never have joined them in killing the prophets.'*

"But in saying that, you testify against yourselves that you are indeed the descendants of those who murdered the prophets. Go ahead and finish what your ancestors started. **Snakes! Sons of vipers! How will you escape the judgment of hell?"**

Now I ask you, do these good ol' boys sound like they are following Jesus or mounting a promotional campaign for that old two-faced, deceiving devil?

In other words, the hypocrite says one thing but does another. I finally understand my grandmother's saying, "It's like putting lipstick on a pig!" The hypocrites love to be seen as "righteous" but are living a lie. They wear two faces, live two lives, and are nothing more than actors on a stage, only wanting to be seen as something that they really aren't. A hypocrite is a fake and someone who does a whole lot of gum-bumping. In a nutshell, I don't consider that someone putting on a mask and pretending is an authentic follower of Christ. And because of that, I most certainly don't think an authentic Christian should be labeled a hypocrite when they fall short of the glory of God. Bear with me!

Well, there's no point in closing the barn door since I've already left it wide open and let the horses out, so let me try to sweep up this mess. Even though authentic Christians are not hypocrites because they aren't putting on a mask, I most certainly accept as true that they are capable of hypocrisy. Authentic Christians can, do and will sometimes act in a fashion contrary to the belief we profess, as well as look down on others when we ourselves are imperfect and doing the very same thing we accuse them of. (That's a whole other conversation.) Yes, a Jesus-loving, fully devoted follower of Christ is capable of sin and will fall, sometimes even jump to the other side of God's protective fence. But if we as Christians are His, and we've surrendered our life, junk in the trunk, closet full of skeletons and all to our Lord, Savior, and King, Jesus and the Holy Spirit has taken up residence in us, then you can take it to the bank that it won't be long after our fence jumping detour before tears are streaming down our faces and running on our knees to the loving, forgiving and safe protection of our heavenly Father's merciful arms, while crying out for our Abba Daddy's forgiveness, as well as others if need be.

WARNING: It's important to always remember that God knows the heart and we are not the judge. But we are also called to produce fruit and recognize those by the fruit produced from being in step with the Holy Spirit. Lack of the fruit of the spirit (Galatians 5:23-23), obedience (John 14:15), faith without works, conviction, and repentance that leads to change, not just of mind but of direction, should make us scratch our head and wonder if some folks have horns holding up their halos and just whose bed are their boots really under. Or for lack of better words, which side of the fence they are living on? Just sayin'!

I think that it is funny—not funny ha-ha—that we desire free will, the freedom to choose, which God out of his pure love for us has so graciously granted, but when someone exercising that God given freedom chooses to jump the protective fence of God's will and run us or someone we love down in the process, we yell and question the character and existence of God. Maybe I am a taco short of a combination plate, but I don't think we have the right or a good reason to blame or be angry at God when anyone chooses to go against the desires of God's heart by packing their bags and vacationing on the other side of His will. I think it's time to put a cork in that pistol and aim the blame back at where and on whom it belongs. Can I get an amen!

I won't get into how it all came about, at least not right now, but at age 37 God reached down into the center of my pitiful life full of turmoil, hurt, pain, and emptiness in a way that so clearly was God. I was guided to a church where the truth of God's word was communicated, and my heart dropped to its knees as I bowed before my Jesus and surrendered my all to my Savior, Lord, and King. Once again, I will make known my ignorance by saying that I assumed or expected each person in the physical structure of the church would be like Jesus. Maybe it was to my benefit that in the beginning stages of my life in Christ that I was ignorant of the in-fighting and disputes that can now and again take place within the church filled with imperfect people.

I am so grateful that when I yielded my life to Christ that I had two formidable Jesus-loving, Jesus-representing people come alongside me and school me in the importance of getting in the word of God and getting the word of God in me. My sweet friends, Robin and Johnny, made sure I was firmly grounded by instructing me that my faith was in Christ and Christ alone. Honest-to-Pete I would have scampered away, just like I did at seventeen, had it not been for the time they spent with me teaching and modeling for me the importance of a foundation of faith built upon the truth, love, promises, faithfulness, strength, hope, and power of my Abba Daddy. They made a point of stressing the importance of me building my house on the solid rock of God's faithfulness.

Trust me, they were so patient, loving, and kind to me as a newborn babe in Christ. I had very little church background to speak of and I was chockfull of questions which were genuinely childlike and yes, ever so often, ignorant. In fact, a few months into my brand-new walk with my Jesus, I was settled in on the front row pew of my new church home, worshipping my awe-inspiring Savior with my adopted family of God and Miss Robin by my side when the worship team began to lead the congregation in singing the song, "All Hail the Power of Jesus Name." When I surrendered my life to Christ, I immersed myself into knowing my Heavenly Father and just couldn't get enough of studying His word. So, as we began to sing the lyrics to the old hymn that everyone, including Miss Robin, seemed to be very familiar with, I was a bit taken aback by one line in the song, that said, "Let angels prostrate fall." I sensed I needed some crucial schooling on the matter at hand, so I leaned over to patient, loving, gentle, and unsuspecting Miss Robin and whispered in her ear, "I didn't think angels had prostrates." (God's word says they don't marry so I assumed . . . no need! Too much information, but I just wanted to give you a tour of my big brain.)

Her eyes got as large as saucers and there on the front pew, in front of God, Pastor Johnny, and everybody else, she started to shake with controlled gut-wrenching laughter. Now mind you she had managed to keep a fairly tight lid on it as long as she could muster, but when she glanced into my ignorant, dazed, and questioning face and realized I was as serious as a heart attack it was all she could do to calmly squeeze out, "Miss Kathy, that's prostate. Prostrate means to fall down." (Oh! Another word I was ignorant of that needed adding to my already growing vocabulary arsenal!)

Well, I reckon the look of shock on my face when I realized what I had just asked was all it took for the last ounce of her self-control to fade and the bottled-up laughter to seep out. Good gravy, anyone who took the notion to look over at us that morning, with our heads huddled close together, hands clenched tight, shoulders shaking, and tears flowing from our eyes would have thought we were praying intensely over some sort of heavy burden. We sat on that pew, through the whole sermon attempting to control our laughter and at times absolutely failing. It still makes me giggle!

You know in the moment of my naïve and ignorant questioning; Miss Robin could have so easily vaulted the fence of God's protective will and chastised me and sent me crying but instead she lovingly taught me. Albeit through barely controlled laughter and tears! Her sweet relationship with our Lord has always helped her to see others through His eyes and love others with His heart and if need be, just laugh with them in their ignorance.

Now I'd be piddling down your back and telling you it's raining if I said that I haven't had instances where those who call themselves Christians, the called-out ones, have not been so Christlike.

Truth is I've been in oodles of head-on collisions, where I was thrashed, mangled, and left for dead as the result of someone's fence jumping. Goodness, mercy me, the scars from being chewed up, spit out, and stepped on can and still do open up and bleed tears every now and then. If not for the profound truth that I not only grasped but have experienced in my life of my ever-loving, almighty, and faithful Abba Daddy and the hope that can only be found in Him I would have thrown in the towel and blown this pop stand called life.

When I handed my life over to Christ, I surrendered all of me to love all of Him. I was then and still am, all in! God in His faithfulness gave me gifts that I understood I was accountable to Him to use, and trust me it was God, for no way, no how, did I have the confidence or education to do the things on my own that God has and is doing in and through me. How could I say no to my Abba Daddy! He has spiritually and literally saved my life! I love Him more than my heart can hold in sometimes! And I most assuredly do not want to be like Jonah who ran away from God's will only to end up in a gigantic fish that later regurgitated him out onto land. Man, that just turns my stomach inside out! Ewww, yuck, and ouch!

What I have come to experience is that when we position our lives in His all-knowing, more-than-capable hands and are willing to go wherever He calls us we put ourselves on the frontline and in the line of fire of a lot of well-aimed and stray bullets. Trust me; you never know what direction the bullets will come from! Being a woman in ministry has been one of the most rewarding and yet painful experiences of my journey, but loving and serving my God was and is weightier and more valuable than the approval of man. My desire to serve my God in whatever capacity He has called and equipped me in, despite my gender, has placed me in the path of several fence jumpers' destructive, unloving words, attitudes, and actions. I am not saying that as Christians we can't or shouldn't disagree with others or voice our opinions, but I do wish that how we do it would always be with the same attitude, mind, and love of Christ Jesus.

A month of Sundays ago I came face to face with the truth that in some way or another along my unpredictable adventure with my Lord I had permitted the heart-rending hit-n-runs, harsh comments, insensitive reactions, and inconsiderate deeds of others hedge me in! So much so that I had tucked my crazy-for-Jesus' heart in and gave up being audacious for Him.

But God . . .

It was around my twentieth year of devotedly serving my Savior that I was working in my office when there came an unanticipated knock on my office door. I was taken back a bit when I opened the door to see a sweet friend, Miss Marie, cheery and biting at the bit to chew the fat with me. She asked if we could talk for a bit and of course, I said yes as I am not one to turn down a good jawing. Usually when somebody would come to my office to talk it would be to chat about details of their ministry or talk over life struggles, they were battling. I was pleasantly surprised that Marie had dropped by, but I was also a bit knocked off balance when my unexpected friend began to solicit my opinion on my competence and expertise at building a wall. Of course, anyone who is familiar with me will say I am crafty in an effective and good way, but I have never erected a wall! I let her in on the fact that masonry was most definitely not up my alley. Yet she was adamant in asserting that she was positive I was more than capable of building a perfectly sound wall. Unyielding, I denied that I had ever erected a wall, nor did I know how to! (I promise this is not meant to be political) That's when her perceptive, honest, and loving comment completely blindsided me, "But Kathy you are very good at building a wall. In fact, you have built one! I miss your hugs and smiles."

She then launched into filling me in on what she knew to be true of my close encounters of the worst kind in ministry and the church and her uneasiness with how she had witnessed it emotionally and spiritually impact my heart. She confessed that the very night before God had aroused her from a deep sleep and laid me on her heart and prompted her to pen words that she was compelled to share with me right then and there. So right there, smack dab in the middle of my everyday routine, I encountered the extraordinary power of God's love, what I like to call a Holy-Now moment, as my gentle Christ-representing friend, in obedience to and out of love for God, confronted me in love with the precious, God-honoring, building-up attitude of Christ as she began to read to me . . .

Kathy
Is not unkind.
Is not boastful.
Is not self-serving.
Is not power-seeking.
Is not untrustworthy.
Is not proud.
Is not uncooperative.
Is not unfriendly.
Is not unwilling.
Is not unhelpful.
Is not impatient.
Is not inconsiderate.
Is not distrustful.
Is not dramatic.
Is not impractical.
Is not quick-tempered.
Is not thoughtless.
Is not unreliable.
Is NEVER unloving!
Kathy is my friend, and I love her for all that she is-not!
But God . . .

Exodus 14:14 New International Version (NIV) — *"The* LORD *will fight for you; you need only to be still."*

Just like that, right when I needed it the most and didn't even know it, right when all the debilitating words and actions of my past and present were rearing their ugly head and pulling me under, right when I was questioning if I was in fact a no-good little girl deserving of abuse, right when I was crying out to God and pondering whether I was a stumbling block or a stepping stone for His kingdom, didn't my Abba Daddy, my faithful, loving, all-knowing God send bold and brave Marie to meet me head-on about my wall-building ways, and in such a way that blessed my heart and made my Jesus smile!

She was on a God mission to speak truth against the lies that had risen and threatened to take root in my heart! With every word she spoke,

I could hear the pounding of God's chisel of love and grace strike the wall I had unknowingly built to protect myself from any more hurt and pain. She was his mouthpiece, an instrument used by God in a time and place when I needed it most. Truth-be-told the wall I had erected to protect myself was doing more harm than good for not only did it keep others at a distance and cause me to doubt the woman God had so fearfully and wonderfully made but it had also shut out the precious, priceless, sweet, loving pure voice of my Abba Daddy.

If God had written me a letter on that day, I believe it would have said this:

I Am the one who has loved you from before the day you were born. Your mama and your daddy may have deserted you, but I will never leave nor forsake you, for you are mine, and **I Am** your Abba Daddy! When you walk through the fire, I will be with you. When you pass through the waters, which I know you are so deathly afraid of, you will not be overwhelmed. I love your love for me and that you are so very willing to go wherever I lead, even when it hurts. I see your tears and hear your weeping in the night, and I will restore to you what the locusts have eaten! I see you and I know your heart and I get you! **I Am** the God of angel armies, and **I Am** fighting for you! That is enough! **I Am** the one who called you by your name on that dark night when you were lying on the bathroom floor weeping, frightened, lost, alone, and giving up on life. **I Am** the one who drew you with loving-kindness to Myself and to the truth you so needed to take notice of, about my precious Son Jesus, who delivered up His life for you. **I Am** the one who reached down into your life of brokenness to redeem you from the pit of despair and hopelessness and brought those dry bones of yours to life again. **I Am** the one that gave you a new name and a new heart! **I Am** the One who sees, hears, and knows all things! **I Am** God, the creator of all things and I don't make junk! **I Am** the one who adopted you! And you, my daughter, are mine forever. Nothing and no one can separate us! You make me smile, cry, laugh, and shake my head, but you have never, nay ever, caused Me not to love you! You are a message to those who exist in this broken world without hope, without peace, without Me, that **I Am** the God who saves and restores! Don't give up for I will never give up on you! Remember that I knitted you in your mother's womb and you are fearfully and wonderfully made. So, stop looking around! Look up and keep your eyes on me! I love you! **I Am** God and I approve this message that you are!

I am so grateful for Miss Marie, my messenger from God, and her love for me as well as her faithfulness and obedience to Him. Isn't it just like our Heavenly Father, that even when we don't realize it and have plugged our ears and built a wall to protect ourselves, He steps in and does something truly miraculous to break down that wall? I love that my God loves me that much! It still makes me cry!

I guess the truth I'm trying to get across is that no matter who is unfaithful to Him in your life it will never alter the fact that He is faithful! When others wound you, and they will, He knows, and He sees. I love the scripture that says that God stores our tears in a bottle. I can't even see in my mind's eye the tear cellar He had to manufacture just to accommodate my tear bottles alone. He is not the One we should get outraged with and run from. He is the One we need to be running to!

Psalm 118:8 New King James Version (NKJV) — *"It is better to trust in the LORD than to put confidence in man."*

Maybe I should hide behind my mama's apron before I ask, but I'm just going to let it fly! Why are we so easily convinced or deceived to think that just because someone goes to church, puts on their fancy britches, speaks all those big Bible names, and perfectly quotes scripture left and right that they will never wound us? Bless our hearts! Trust me, I am preaching to myself as well! Just because a chicken has wings doesn't mean it can fly! Don't even get me started on the topic of buffalo wings, y'all!

In the church you will come across many authentic Christians who are so sold out to Jesus that if a mosquito bites them, it will start singing there is power in the blood! But as authentic as they are, they are imperfect souls loving a perfect God and will fall short and miss God's holy mark on their best day.

And as sure as I'm sitting here you will also encounter some bona fide hypocrites, donning their masks, going through the motions, and putting their best act forward for all the wrong reasons.

And then there are the unbelievers who are searching for Jesus and hoping to catch a glimpse of Jesus in those that say they are following Him. Listen, we need to recognize that our faith is not in people, no matter which side of the fence they stand on or straddle for that matter! And all are capable of sinning and hurting us!

Now by no means, no-how, and no shape or form am I endorsing or giving free license to the redeemed folk, those that are His, to act hitched but not churched. As the called-out ones, we have a responsibility to our Savior to shine brightly for Him. Hallelujah! Our faith is in a living, holy, faithful, and merciful God and we best be about our Father's business.

I was teaching an adult Sunday school class when a couple that had been absent for about six weeks walked in. I, being the humorous person that I tend to be, strode over to them and asked their name like they were new to the church. Well, it was about 15 minutes into the lesson when the wife of the couple I had joked around with stormed out of the class crying. After quickly excusing myself from the group I went to check on her and found her in the ladies' bathroom weeping uncontrollably. My heart sank and ached for her pain. So, I tried to wrap my arms around her which she made clear she wanted no part of. I asked her if she had been hurt by someone in our group and she came back with a big adamant yes. When I gently implored her to tell me who had hurt her feelings, she confessed that it was I who had inflicted the pain she was expressing. I was so devastated by the realization that something I had said or done had hurt her. To be honest I wasn't even sure what I had said to cause her to be so distraught! When I questioned her as to how I had wounded her she heatedly responded,

"By drawing attention to me when I walked into the room!"

Even though I was a little taken aback by her answer and slightly relieved that I had not intentionally inflicted harm on her, I grieved the pain she was feeling and asked her to please forgive me. Without even a thought she told me she couldn't forgive me, stormed out of the bathroom, seized her quiet husband, and marched out the church doors, never to return. Her response and refusal to forgive me broke my heart and honest-to-Pete it was a good long while before I could joke with anyone for fear of that very same reaction.

Truth-be-told, we will, and we do cause pain to each other, unintentionally and sometimes intentionally. And honestly, sometimes people who have been bitten bite back! No matter who is doing the biting or why we are still responsible for our response! And we need to pray for a Holy Spirit muzzle to keep us from biting in return.

All that to say whether we like it or not, the world comes into the church! But isn't that what we want? But Christian, we need to remember we are not to be like the world! How will the world ever know or see the difference Jesus makes if we aren't the difference we teach and preach? The body of Christ's job is to bring people hope, hope that can only be found in Jesus. We are not perfect, and we will sin; that is true! But that should never be an excuse to deliberately, unashamedly, climb over the protective fence of God's will and dance on it like we just don't care.

If we are going to bear our Savior's brand, wave His banner, and claim to love Him with all our heart, soul, mind, strength, and oomph then we had best be displaying our Savior's heart and mind and be the sermon before we preach it! People are sometimes more influenced by what they see than what they hear and if we, the gathered community of Christ followers, the redeemed from the pit folk, unbound from the shackles of sin saints and saved by amazing grace sinners aren't gonna walk the talk and talk the walk then this might be a good time to not miss the chance to sit down and shut up!

John 13:34-35 New International Version (NIV) — *"A new command I give you: Love one another. As I have loved you, so you must love one another. By this everyone will know that you are my disciples, if you love one another."*

Need Jesus say more!

What the world needs right now is to know the love of Jesus Christ, and to see those who say they are following Christ act like they know the love of Jesus Christ. Can I get a witness!

I will be the first to raise my hand and say that there are times that I have failed miserably in representing my Jesus. I have at one time or another, been the poster child for exactly the opposite. Our problem might be that we think loving others is based on a feeling of love when God is commanding us to love one another whether we feel like it or not. Hoot, there it is!

Here is what I know, based on the truth of God's word. Jesus died for me, not because I deserved it, not because I was loveable or even loving Him back, but because He loved and acted in love despite the life I was living apart from Him. It's time for us as followers of Christ, to get off our pews and represent the King!

We had a Vietnamese exchange student reside with us as part of a foreign student exchange program. During his time with us, he began to behave very badly. After several incidents with him, his parents contacted us to apologize for his bad behavior and ask for our forgiveness. They were so disheartened and angry that the young man was not representing his family in a way that brought them honor.

Do we represent our Savior, our King, and Our heavenly Father in a way that gives Him honor?

Do you know, do you understand
that you represent Jesus to me?
Do you know, do you understand
that when you treat me with gentleness,
it raises the question in my mind
that maybe He is gentle, too?
Maybe He isn't someone who laughs when I am hurt.
Do you know, do you understand
that when you listen to my questions
and you don't laugh,
I think, "What if Jesus is interested in me, too?"
Do you know, do you understand
that when I hear you talk honestly about arguments
and conflict and scars from your past
that I think, "Maybe I am just a regular person

instead of a bad, no-good little girl who deserves abuse."
If you care, I think maybe He cares—
and then there's this flame of hope
that burns inside of me
and for a while, I am afraid to breathe
because it might go out.
Do you know, do you understand
that your words are His words?
Your face is His face to someone like me?
Please—be who you say you are.
Please, God, don't let this be another trick.
Please let this be real. Please!
Do you know, do you understand
That you represent Jesus to me? (Author Unknown)

This poem shattered my heart and made my eyes leak when I first read it. Oh, how I identified with the emotions and thoughts of the girl that echoed throughout the poem, a little too much if I might add. But it also served as a reminder of the weight of being who I say I am, an ambassador of Jesus Christ, to those who were where I used to be. Who knows, maybe I would have become a follower of Christ sooner rather than later, if I had seen one. But then again, I can't hang my wash on someone else's line, can I! Just sayin'!

To all of those precious representatives of Christ (and there have been and are many) who are a sermon before they preach one, who talk the talk, walk the walk, and who have been the arms, words, actions, heart, and face of Jesus; I just want to wrap you in a big Texas hug and say thank you from the bottom of my redeemed and ever-thankful heart! You smell like Jesus to me, and I am blessed. You know who you are! I love you to the moon and back!

John 13:34-35 (NLT) — *"So now I am giving you a new commandment: Love each other. Just as I have loved you, you should love each other. Your love for one another will prove to the world that you are my disciples."*

When we say we love Jesus, and we inflict pain on others in any shape, form, or fashion, we as Christians should be the first to own up to failings. We should also be the first to forgive whether they say they are sorry or not! And when, not if, it happens that you should be on the receiving end of someone's fence jumping, I hope you remember that God sees and acts. He will not forget you! He will fight on your behalf! For He is the world-creating, life-breathing, star-producing, gate-guarding, pit-redeeming, roof-crashing, water-walking, river-parting, storm-ceasing, truth-delivering, lifesaving, always faithful, holy and unchanging God. When someone intentionally or unintentionally leaps the protective fence of God's will please don't run from God, run to Him! And for goodness' sake don't hang your wash on someone else's line. Our faith, hope, joy, and peace are not meant to be in one another, but in Him and Him alone! Our walk with Him is based on who He is and not who others are or are not! Thank you, Jesus! He's got this! We'd do well to remember that! Trust me, I know! Better yet, trust Him!

And for God's sake, for His holy name Christian, wherever you may wander, please remember you are filled with the Holy Spirit, so please be the church!

1 Corinthians 3:16-17 The Message (MSG) — *"You realize, don't you, that you are the temple of God, and God himself is present in you? No one will get by with vandalizing God's temple, you can be sure of that. God's temple is sacred—and you, remember, are the temple."*

God has given you everything you need to walk in His way and by His power!

I read a story of a man who took his daughter to a carnival. Upon entering, the little girl immediately rushed to the booth and asked for cotton candy. As the attendant handed her a huge ball of it the father asked, "Sweetheart, are you sure you can eat all of that candy?"

"Don't worry, Dad," she answered. "I'm a lot bigger on the inside than I am on the outside."

1 John 4:4 — *"He who is in you is greater than he who is in the world."*

We are much bigger on the inside than on the outside! Remember you are a temple of the Holy Spirit!

And if you are reading this and have used someone's fence jumping or maybe your own fence vaulting as a defense to turn your back on God and to not be part of His body of Christ, please turn around before you find yourself in the belly of a fish. Stop running from the only One that can truly redeem your life from the pit. Just like the prodigal son who came to his senses and returned home, you can do the same. You can choose right now to run toward Him and fall into His waiting arms. He loves you beyond words, even to death on the cross. Trust me! Better yet, trust Him! Don't hang your wash on someone else's line. Church is out! Or is it!

CHAPTER THREE

DANCING IN THE HOG TROUGH

Faster than a rat up a drainpipe, my Sunday morning went from joyful expectancy of the day's worship events to me pitching a hissy fit times four and being as nervous as a fly in a glue pot. Let me tell you, that never, nay ever, could I have reckoned that when I arrived at church that fine-looking Sunday morning, I would be accosted by a suspiciously out-of-place snake, no bigger than a minnow in a fishing pond, taking a break on the cold concrete floor directly in my footpath.

It did ever so briefly cross my mind, because of my practical joker ways and the snakes' lack of movement, that this could well be a new tactic by my cunning pastor to serve up a little retaliation for the countless, albeit innocent but impeccably timed practical jokes I had carried out on him over the past several years. Undisruptive and trifling little pranks like; battery-operated fish in the baptismal; decorating the outside of his house with Christmas lights and all the trimmings during the dog days of summer while he and his family were vacationing; fabricating what gave the impression of a very believable homicide scene in his driveway, decked out with crime scene tape, a chalk outline of a dead body and a small number of other convincing essentials; depositing a harmless little rubber snake in his office desk drawer and my favorite of all my practical capers; arranging my painstakingly folded clothes along with the church mail on the floor outside my office door in such a way that he would start to suspect that the rapture had come to pass and question if he had been left behind. If anything, I should get a pat on the back for creativity and gumption! Oh, the stories I could share, but I won't!

It's a fact, that even though I hail from the grand ol' country of Texas the birthright blessing that was bestowed upon me did not make me double-backboned and gutsy enough to stick around long enough to determine whether a snake was real or not. My common sense and scaredy-cat way of doing business with anything that bore any resemblance to a serpent is to cut loose and run faster than a scalded cat in the other direction. If I had my druthers, I think I'd rather charge hell with a bucket of ice water than take my chances with a snake!

Yet, something just didn't sit right about this snake. After taking stock of what I thought was a dire situation and observing how utterly stock-still the snake was, I, in my know-how as a snake-ologist by Texas birthright, deduced that if it didn't act like a snake, then it must not be a bona fide genuine snake. So matter-of-factly, and without any thought in my big brain I audaciously stooped down to take a firm grip on the harmless and counterfeit-looking snake, with all the not-so-noble intention of hiding it somewhere new for some unfortunate, gullible, and unsuspecting victim to happen upon. I know! Just being truthful, y'all!

Well, I swanee', don't you know that the moment I got near enough to get chummy and pluck up the harmless little serpent didn't it commence to squirm and slither away from me and across the floor. In that moment, as my life flashed before my eyes, my built-in alert warning system was triggered and on high-alert mode didn't I begin to hoot and holler to anyone within range of my high-pitched voice that there was an honest-to-goodness snake in the fellowship hall. But even after saying the safe word, trust me, no one would believe me and come to my aid. So, I ran in the direction of the pastor's office in the hopes of convincing him that there was a snake in the church. Needless to say, but I'll say it anyway, he didn't believe me either. Hmmm, I wonder why! It wasn't till I used the safe word, trust me, that he rolled his eyes, stood up, and said, "Okay Miss Kathy, where is the snake?"

After his mistrusting attitude, you can bet the farm on it that I got a whole mess of satisfaction when Pastor Johnny confidently leaned down without hesitation to gather up the snake that he had already deemed another one of my practical jokes and wound up running away faster than a sneeze through a front door when the snake began to move! Just the thought of it still makes me giggle! He's a hardcore devil stomping pastor and they don't startle so easily.

Let me just get down to the nitty gritty here and warn you right now! There is a snake in the road of this thing we call life, and he wants us to think he isn't real, or better yet, he is harmless. And in case you have had your head under a rock and don't know, he is more slippery than a pocketful of pudding and so crooked he has to unscrew his britches at night. He will take a lie, twist and dress it up so that it appears mouthwatering and enticing, so much so that you will talk yourself into supposing that there is no harm, no foul in sampling just one tiny little bite. And the second you begin to feel comfortable with gorging on the slop from his stinky hog trough of lies and deception is also the instant you just might discover that pigs get fat but hogs, well, they just get slaughtered.

I don't think I can emphasize enough that he is such a liar he'd beat you senseless and tell God you fell off a horse. He is so low that one day he will have to look up to see hell and guess what; his goal is to take us with him. I think you get my point! Our hugest mistake, whether it be out of ignorance, denial, or out-and-out stupidity, is not being familiar with or recognizing his rascally ways. Some even find comfort in the notion that he will most assuredly whistle before he walks into their camp. Shucks, even the chickens under the porch know that dog won't hunt. And if you think he is dead then just remember this; even a dead snake can still bite. He is as dark as the inside of a wolf and as slick as cat poop on linoleum. And that is putting it nicely, y'all!

I reckon that ignorance or denial just might be the common denominator in us not spotting or distinguishing the truth from a lie or the real from the counterfeit when we lay our eyes upon it. We may set our eyes and heart on something destructive but because we just don't recognize the difference between good and evil or we hanker something so badly that the truth no longer carries any weight in our decision-making, we choose to pluck it up anyway, all the while not taking into account the piercing fangs, incessant rattling, and toxic venom as we take it home with us to be our family pet. We provide it with a roof over its deluding head, a dwelling place to settle in for a spell, and sustenance for its insatiable belly. And even when our toxic companion from hell rears its foul head, attacks, and wounds us and those we love, time and time again, we just choose to continue to look the other way, all the while making it more hazardous, as we fatten it up for the kill by supplying it with a never-ending diet of acceptance, tolerance, rationalization and/or justification. We breastfeed it so thoroughly and frequently, that one day we notice to our astonishment, that not only has it made itself comfy and cozy by taking up full residence in our heart, its home, but that it has staked its claim to every inch of our life and grown as fat and content as a boarding house cat. It's then that we realize the tables have turned and we have not only become its caged prized pet but also an all-you-can-eat buffet that it pigs out on.

We are in a war and our biggest hindrance in being victorious is that we don't always recognize the enemy hiding behind the seemingly harmless snake. The day Adam and Eve entertained the serpent's question in Genesis 3:3, "But did God really say," is the day it all went to hell in a handbasket with gasoline panties on.

We are quicker to give an audience to and take the gussied-up word of the devil himself, Facebook, Google, the world, and anyone and everything other than listen to our heavenly Father! By no means am I declaring that we have men and women out there who teach and preach that aren't standing on the truth of God's word and aren't worthy to listen to. Even Paul said, "Follow me as I follow Christ"! We just need to make certain that the ones we are seeking counsel from are following Christ and the only way to do that is to know the difference between the truth and a lie.

Cause if they aren't following Jesus and we begin to shadow them, well we could end up like the guy who was following GPS instructions to the Grand Canyon, not questioning the condition of the roads he was on or the lack of roads for that matter, only to end up at his final destination and driving off into a canyon. I have nothing against GPS, but it just cracks me up that we just take so much at face value without checking under the hood. We wouldn't dare purchase a car in that manner!

I'm just sayin' we need to check to see that what we are being told is from the word of God and not the lies of Satan. We need to ask, "What does God say?" If we don't know the difference between the truth and the lie when God has made it as plain as a pig on a sofa, then how in the world are we going to stroll away from this life without getting skinned and eaten alive? If you haven't noticed, the devil is in the business of stealing your joy, killing your relationship with our Lord and Savior and others, and hell-bent on destroying your witness. And he doesn't rest! Any season for him is hog-killing weather. We need to stop dancing in the hog trough!

My husband sometimes teases me when I share a thought-provoking fact (I use that word loosely) that I acquired from Facebook by saying, "Well, if it's on Facebook, it must be the truth!"

Don't tell him I said this, but he is often right. Just because someone crows it doesn't necessarily mean the sun is up. Just because it's on Facebook doesn't mean it's a fact!

And we can never assume that there are no consequences to dancing in the hog trough. Even a blind man on a galloping horse can see that. If you read the first chapter of this book, then you are all too familiar with the side effects I suffered because of truth deprivation and decay. Those consequences transferred over into my children's lives and now influence my grandchildren. Yes, I know I was young, but I can't say that I was ignorant of the fact that the word of God existed. When the church I attended began to preach about Jesus coming back on a specific day, I should have looked under the hood and checked the owner's manual, the Word of God, as should everyone in that church. We all make choices, but I do think some may have the notion that it is more convenient, loving, or comfortable to believe the lie. It didn't work out so well for the gullible man who unsuspectingly drove off the cliff all because he didn't examine the map to authenticate that the directions GPS gave him were true.

Someone once stated that the definition of insanity is doing the same thing over and over while expecting a different result. Recently I heard someone say that insanity is when we believe the lie! I want to take it one step further and say insanity is when we don't bother to know the difference between the lie and the truth! Ignorance is not bliss! Trust me, I know! Some of our choices have a lifetime of consequences. We deceive ourselves if we reckon it will all come out in the wash! We best not tip over the outhouse by blaming someone else for what we are reaping because of our choice to dance in the hog trough instead of drinking from the well of living water. If we think that the word of God is an accessory and not a necessity, then we have most assuredly lost our vertical hold. Cross my heart and hope to spit!

When I was around the seasoned old age of seventeen, I worked in the office of a lumber yard, logging invoices received from the shipping and receiving department in the back. One day the good ol' boys in receiving supposed it would be a rib-tickling moment to deposit a very lively and deadly-looking snake in the air tube through which the invoices were sent back to my desk. Now and until the day the music died, and they took it upon themselves to send me ye old sneaky snake, I had never entertained the notion that I would need to be on my guard and expect anything other than an invoice being in that air tube. You can only imagine my reaction when I naively snapped open the harmless air tube and reached my hand in to grab the invoice but instead got up close and personal with a thirty-foot boa constrictor. (In that moment it might as well have been one, y'all.)

I admit I'm not as country as cornflakes, cause the moment I snatched hold of that serpent you would have assumed that someone was scalding a cat by the shrieks that rang throughout the building. Why even the good ol' boys in the receiving department came running out of concern that they might have just given me a heart attack. Of course, once they realized I was alive and kicking, although barely, they launched into fits of knee-slapping laughter, hooting, and hollering. Bless their hearts!

That night I went home and concocted a simple plan to convey my appreciation to those good ol' boys in receiving in a like manner, and with something befitting the tears-running-down-my-leg fright they had so kindly bestowed upon me. Yes, indeedy, I prepared them a deliciously rich, moist, and yummy, chocolate cake, crowned with saliva-inducing, decadently sweet and creamy, chocolate Ex-Lax frosting. Yes, I admit I have a thinking problem! I know that the retribution I was dishing out wasn't quite as fitting for the crime but in what seemed like a harmless and satisfying moment of payback, I didn't even have the sense to spit downwind. Just sayin'!

So, the next morning I sashayed back to the unsuspecting good ol' boys in the receiving department, a big, sweet innocent-looking smile plastered on my face, holding what seemed to be the sweetest, most delectable, mouth-watering chocolate cake you had ever sank your teeth into. The good ol' boys were so taken aback by my kind-heartedness and goodwill that you could have knocked them over with a powder puff. Truth-be-told I was beginning to feel a wee bit guilt-ridden, but I got over it in one-half less than no time. After my short-lived battle with what is upright and what is wicked, I offered those good ol' boys their just desserts and assured them that I was raring to forgive and forget, and just wished to let the dust settle by baking them a cake. Yes, I did that! Can I use the defense that this vigilante action of mine was BC, before Christ, or that I just was ignorant of the outcome of what wolfing down a box of Ex-lax would do to a fellow? Hmmm, I reckon not!

Well, any hoot the next morning when I drove into the parking lot at work, I could tell something was terribly cattywampus. As I soaked in my surroundings, I was truly flabbergasted and taken aback to see not one or two but several plumbing trucks taking up spaces in the lumber yard parking lot. When I entered the building, I was shocked to see everyone jumping around like hot grease in a skillet. My boss was running (pardon the pun) around like a chicken with his head cut off, cursing to high heaven about all the commodes being backed up and that half of the receiving department, the good ol' boys had called out sick with the runs. Although it might be questionable, I wasn't born yesterday, and I reckoned there was no time like the present to make like a banana and split. I kid you not, as sure as I'm sitting here, I never went back, even for my last paycheck. I just couldn't risk going to jail for giving all those good ol' boys the runs. So, I ran!

I've been in the idiot relocation program ever since! My mama didn't raise no fool! Shucks, this is the first time I've put into writing the details of my good-girl-gone-bad-lax-sound-judgment chocolate incident for fear that one of those boys, who fell victim to my stupidity and lax morals that day would track me down and open up a can of much deserved whoop on me!

All that to say is that we, myself included, are way too hasty, when we set our eyes or hearts on something, to make an assumption that there is no harm in it, based purely on its appearance, packaging, or our hankering for it. Shucks, most of the time we don't even bother to check the ingredients, which just might save our lives, nor question the motive of the one presenting it to us. It's more about whatever greases our wagon than whether an axle is missing.

John 10:10a (NIV) — "*The thief comes only to steal and kill and destroy.*"

That deceiving devil/snake in the road will gussie up his lying propaganda in such a mouth-watering bundle, tidy it up so lovely with his twisting of words, all the while appealing to our desires, so that we begin to question God as to why we can't have our cake and eat it too. (Sorry, I just couldn't resist!) Maybe we should be scratching our heads and camping on the fact that the devil just might have an end game in mind! He wants you and I to get the runs! Bear with me! Remember Jonah, who instead of doing God's will ran, right into the blood-soaked mouth, down the flesh-greased esophagus, and into the belly of a big man-eating fish. Jonah got the runs and when the whale regurgitated him out onto land, I bet he looked and smelled like he had been inside an outhouse when lightning struck. That's what the runs will do to you, whether it is out of ignorance, defiance of the will of God, or an encounter with a redhead bent on revenge. (I'm trying, y'all.) Lax judgment will cause you to end up on the run! (Oops I did it again!)

Deception can come in so many different forms, shapes, and sizes. I'll never forget the time I sunk my teeth into the most incredible school cafeteria chocolate brownie I had ever feasted my eyes upon. It looked and tasted so delicious that it wasn't till I was about halfway through the irresistible brownie that I took notice of something quite peculiar. Right smack dab in the middle of the best school cafeteria brownie I had ever sunk my teeth into, the kind of brownie that dreams are made of and that I had been hankering for all morning long, was a big brown gag-inducing worm! Oh, but here is where the truth hits the fan, y'all! I had been so bent on getting my gratification that not only had I eaten half the brownie, without coming up for air I might add, but I had also eaten half the worm, too! If that don't put a hitch in your git-along then nothing will! Still makes me a tad sick when I think about it!

2 Corinthians 11:3 (NIV) — "*But I am afraid that just as Eve was deceived by the serpent's cunning, your minds may somehow be led astray from your sincere and pure devotion to Christ.*"

The following quotes seem harmless enough, but we don't want to miss the worm or the snake in the middle, y'all. These are responses from children when asked what the God-breathed word of God says!

- The first commandment was when Eve told Adam to eat the apple. (I laughed too at the thought of a man listening to a woman! Just kidding, y'all—or not!)
- The seventh commandment is thou shalt not admit adultery. (Not even going there!)
- God wants a man to have only one wife. He calls that monotony. (All I can say is they must not be married to a Texan!)
- Lot's wife was a pillar of salt by day, but a ball of fire by night. (Now, that sounds like a Texan!)
- Noah's wife was called Joan of Ark. (The naked truth and just the truth?)
- Solomon, one of David's sons, had 300 wives, and 700 porcupines. (Either way, it sounds painful!)
- Moses died before He reached Texas. (Now this is just sad to the umpteenth power considering God blessed Texas with His own hand!)
- Moses led the Hebrews to the Red Sea, where they made unleavened bread, which is bread without any ingredients. (Is this where the Daniel diet began?)
- The greatest miracle in the bible is when Joshua told his son to stand still, and he obeyed him. (I know every parent just shouted amen, praise the Lord, it's a miracle!)
- Jesus enunciated the Golden Rule, which says to do one to others before they do one to you. (You might want to read that again!)
- Jesus was born because Mary had an immaculate contraption. (Surprise, I'm speechless!)
- Adam and Eve were created from an apple tree. (Hmmm? This one left me out on a limb!)

At first read you just can't help but giggle since it's kids, and they can and often do say the darndest things. Although these little misquotes or misunderstandings may seem harmless enough, I hope you will agree with me when I say that it only takes a little Ex-lax here and a little Ex-lax there before someone is going to get the runs. I'm pretty sure those good ol' boys at the lumber yard would agree with me on that one too! No different than

it only takes a twisting of the truth here or denying of it there before someone will find that while they are fleeing God's presence, they have ended
up on the other side of God's protective will shining the devil's boots and
recruiting members for his fan club. Been there, done that!

Proverbs 19:18 — *"Discipline your children, for in that there is hope; do
not be a willing party to their death."*

When I read about discipline in the word of God it deals with a
Father, including our heavenly Father, steering their child to do what is
right by undergoing physical suffering. But it is the word of God that
gives us the counseling and correction we need so that we don't end up
on the other end of Him having to take us to the holy woodshed and
open up a can of divine whoop on us!

We need to be disciplined about getting in the word of God so that
when the forgery comes our way, we are so submerged in the truth we can
identify the fib. There is a standard, the word of God, by which we as well
as our children should know and learn, so that we don't find ourselves
straddling, falling off, or jumping over the fence of God's shielding and
loving will. Hopefully you didn't miss the part in Proverbs 19:18 where it
says that by not correcting and teaching our children, we become a willing
party to their death. I know we may have all had moments where we said,
"I brought you into this world and I can take you out," but God help us
if we who have been entrusted to teach them the truth and correct their
path choose to ignore our God-given responsibility and become a willing
party to their death, spiritually or physically. If that doesn't give you God
bumps, I don't know what will! I reckon sometimes Jesus just needs to
take off his flip flop and give us a good old-fashioned divine whooping.

2 Timothy 3:16-17 — *"All Scripture is inspired by God and is useful to
teach us what is true and to make us realize what is wrong in our lives. It
corrects us when we are wrong and teaches us to do what is right."*

But lest we start making excuses and giving up alibis for our ignorance of the word of God, God is pretty clear that if we are going to know
where the fence is then we need to be reading the map and training for
righteousness.

Hebrews 9:14 — *"But solid food is for the mature, who by constant use have trained themselves to distinguish good from evil."*

We adults have our library of misleading quotes that we like to throw out there too.

God helps those who help themselves. (Nope, not in the Bible)

Truth: God seeks and wants our reliance on Him.

Proverbs 3:5-6 (NIV) —

Trust in the Lord with all your heart
    and lean not on your own understanding;
in all your ways submit to him,
    and he will make your paths straight.

God never gives you more than you can handle.

If it truly is about what we can handle, then we will either be patting ourselves on the back instead of praising God for what He has done or giving up our last breath because we know we just can't handle it! If you've read the Bible, and I hope you have, then you will see over and over men and women who were given far more than they can handle. Job, Noah, Daniel, Moses, David, Meshach, Shadrach, and the list goes on and on.

Truth: God regularly gives us more than we can handle, for the aim of challenging us to put our trust in Him. Our source of coziness should not be God's holding back, but God Himself.

Now, the Bible says that God won't allow you to be *tempted* beyond your limits, but we might want to read that over and over a couple of times.

1 Corinthians 10:13 — *"No temptation has seized you except what is common to man. And God is faithful; he will not let you be tempted beyond what you can bear. But when you are tempted, he will also provide a way out so that you can stand up under it."*

When tested, God always gives us a way out, His way. The problem is we usually use that as an excuse to do it our way!

Money is the root of all evil.

Truth: The love of money is the root of all evil (**1 Timothy 6:10**).

This too shall pass. (Nope, Nope!)

Truth: God never leaves us, and He will be with us through everything. In this life, there is no guarantee that it will pass. I know we say it to comfort someone but what if you say that to someone and it doesn't pass. Ouch! This saying is based more on our circumstances changing instead of us trusting God in our situation that whether it passes away or not, He is good and He is God.

I've been privy to women who have suffered tremendously because of truth decay, someone saying something about the workings of God that just didn't fit within the context of the word or character of God. Now I don't know if it was out of ignorance, twisting or misinterpretation of the character and will of God, but either way it had an impact on their walk. The following recounts are but only a few but heartbreaking because they are true.

A young girl who didn't believe she was saved because she had been told that if she had the Holy Spirit, the seal of our redemption, she would have a specific gift. (Makes me want to open a can of whoop!)

Ephesians 1:13-14 clears this lie up really quick! *"And you also were included in Christ when you heard the message of truth, the gospel of your salvation. When you believed, you were marked in him with a seal, the promised Holy Spirit, who is a deposit guaranteeing our inheritance until the redemption of those who are God's possession—to the praise of his glory."*

Then there was the mom who was grieving the loss of her teenage son only to be told by some that her young son died of cancer because she didn't have enough faith.

A husband who left his wife because he felt God had given him the okay when he read the scripture that says we shouldn't worry about tomorrow and that it will take care of itself.

Satan is a deceiver and a liar and one of his most effective weapons in his evil tool chest is the twisting of the truth of God's word or the ignorance of those who do not know the difference between God's truth, an untruth, fib, tall tale, or a white lie.

John 17:17 says, *"Your word is truth."*

John 14:16 says, *"I am (Jesus) the way, the truth, the life."*

If it doesn't line up with the character of God and/or is contrary to the word of God, within its context please, then we just might be guilty of standing on sinking sand about as thin as a gnat's whisker as opposed to the firm foundation of God. If we don't stand on the truth, then we will fall for anything!

Be sure of this that God wants his truth to not only be grasped by our minds but also to go deep in our hearts.

Psalm 51:6 — *"Surely you desire truth in the inner parts; you teach me wisdom in the inmost place."*

We need to be knowledgeable about the word of God and know God so intimately, personally, that when, not if, we encounter the snake on the road we travel, we don't find ourselves on the other side of God's loving and protective fence, sick as a dog passing peach pits, trying to mow down the tall stink weeds of our poor decision-making, while headed in the general direction of pushing up daisies. I don't know about you, but I have discovered that I can't always stand on someone else's promises or character, but I will never fall if I am leaning on His.

2 Peter 1:19 — ***And so we have more sure the prophetic word confirmed,*** *(scripture is more complete, more permanent, and more authoritative than the experience of anyone)* **which you do well to heed** *(there will be false teachers and lies; pay attention to scripture)* **as a light that shines in a dark place,** *(God's word is a lamp unto my feet and a light unto my path)* **until the day dawns and the morning star rises in your heart** *(perfect revelation of scripture will be replaced by the perfect revelation of Jesus Christ)* **knowing this first** *(His truth should be priority)* **that no prophecy of Scripture** *(all of scripture)* **is of any private interpretation** *(God's revelation not man's ideas)* **for prophecy never came by the will of man** *(not by human effort, oftentimes prophets wrote what they could not understand)* **but holy men of God spoke as they were moved by the Holy Spirit.**

Now, not always is it ignorance of God's will and character that leads to us entertaining a real live snake. Truth-be-told we can rationalize just about anything until we have convinced ourselves that it is okay.

Honest-to-Pete, we just want what we want when we want it, despite what the word of God declares, and we will make any and every attempt to rationalize our decision. I think one of the statements I've heard used the most to justify someone's trampling on the protective fencing of God's will is, "I was born this way!"

We were all born this way, but we most certainly were not created this way.

Genesis 1:31 — *"God saw all that he had made, and it was very good."*
But then the snake entered the garden . . . Hoot, there it is!

Genesis 3:3 — *"Now the serpent was more crafty than any of the wild animals the Lord God had made. He said to the woman, 'Did God really say, 'You must not eat from any tree in the Garden'?' The woman said to the serpent, 'We may eat fruit from the trees in the garden, but God did say, 'You must not eat fruit from the tree that is in the middle of the garden, and you must not touch it, or you will die.'"*

There are so many things I would love to camp on right now about what I think went wrong in this whole scenario, but I won't. What I would like to unpack is that this could have been sidestepped if Adam and Eve had only trusted and obeyed God, the creator, instead of entertaining the snake's twisted deceptions. You give Satan an inch and he becomes a ruler!

Genesis 3:6 — *"When the woman saw that the fruit of the tree was good for food and pleasing to the eye, and also desirable for gaining wisdom, she took some and ate it. She also gave some to her husband, who was with her, and he ate it."*

Don't miss the chance to notice that what got Adam and Eve into trouble was relying upon their eyes, belly, flesh, and the cunning of a troublemaking, scheming, and sneaking serpent more than the One who had fashioned them and provided for them in the first place. Like someone who can't see the forest for the trees, they couldn't see the Ex-lax or the worm for the hunger pains of their belly and their flesh. I know I need to let that one go, pardon the pun!

Lest we forget . . . **James 1:13**: *"When tempted, no one should say, 'God is tempting me.' For God cannot be tempted by evil, nor does he tempt anyone; but each person is tempted when they are dragged away by their own evil desire and enticed. Then, after desire has conceived, it gives birth to sin; and sin, when it is full-grown, gives birth to death."*

Need God say more! What was good was now bad! What was found was now lost! What was clean was now polluted! What was whole was now broken! What was alive was now dead!

Romans 5:12 — *"When Adam sinned, sin entered the world. Adam's sin brought death, so death spread to everyone, for everyone sinned."*

R.I.F, as my mama used to say whenever she was diagnosed with some new ailment," It runs in the family". So, we inherited sin from Adam just as my granddaughter inherited red hair from me or her stubbornness from her mama. RIF!

Psalm 51:5 — *"Surely, I was sinful at birth, sinful from the time my mother conceived me."*

So yes, baby we were born this way, born to be wild, sinful at birth, because it's R.I.F, runs in family! We were born with a sin nature that seduces us to commit sin.

Romans 3:23 — *"All have fallen short of the glory of God."*

And the consequences . . . what we earn . . .

Romans 6:23 — *"The wages of sin are death, but the gift of God is eternal life, in Christ Jesus."*

The result of our sin nature is that we sin, and this sin separates us from a relationship with a perfect, sinless God.

Isaiah 64:6 — *"We have all become like one who is unclean, and all our righteous deeds are like a polluted garment. We all fade like a leaf, and our iniquities, like the wind, take us away."*

Jesus said that salvation is like being born again.

John 3:5-7 — *"Truly, truly I say to you, unless one is born of water and the Spirit, he cannot enter the kingdom of God. That which is born of flesh is flesh, and that which is born of the Spirit is spirit. Do no marvel that I said to you, 'You must be born again.'"*

But God provided a way for us to receive forgiveness through faith in Jesus Christ. And only Christ can prevail over the sin nature in us.

Ephesians 2:1 — *"And you He made alive, who were dead in trespasses and sin."*

So, when we situate our faith and trust in Jesus Christ, we not only take our lives out of the hands of an idiot and position them into His ever-faithful, all-powerful, loving hands but we are no longer spiritually dead, and we are given spiritual life through faith in Jesus Christ. We are reborn, born all over again of the Spirit and here and now in a right relationship with God all because of the precious atoning work of Jesus Christ.

2 Corinthians 5:17 — *"Therefore, if anyone is in Christ, he is a new creation: the old has gone, the new has come."*

We are no longer slaves to sin! Woo Hoo!

John 1:12-13 — *"Yet to all who received him, to those who believed in his name, he gave the right to become children of God children born not of natural descent, (hoot there it is) nor of human decision or a husband's will but born of God."*

(Hoot there it is)

All this to say that yes, we were born this way, of the flesh, but through Christ, we have been reborn of the spirit so that the flesh no longer has control or power over us. Christians are capable of sin and will sin but as Christians, we can no longer use the excuse, "I was born this way," to blatantly trample on or disregard the holiness of God or justify off-roading on the dark side that goes against His protective will.

Galatians 5:16-17 (NIV) — *"So I say, let the Holy Spirit guide your lives. Then you won't be doing what your sinful nature craves. The sinful nature* *wants to do evil, which is just the opposite of what the Spirit wants. And the Spirit gives us desires that are the opposite of what the sinful nature desires. These two forces are constantly fighting each other, so you are not free to carry out your good intentions."*

A good while back we had a big snowstorm and since the grandkids, who were young'uns, had spent the night at our house and church had been cancelled, I decided we would have church in our home. I was shaken to the core by my grandkids' answers when I asked them how they determine what is right or wrong. Their responses were based more on what feels good, what makes a person happy, and the world's view than the truth of God's word. And they know the truth, y'all!

Faith is not only having confidence that the word of God is true but acting upon that certainty despite feelings, circumstances, culture, or what the world says. I'm not talking about legalism here. I'm talking about a truth that will set you free from the pressure of peers, emotions, culture, etc. We need truth and God has given us absolute truth, His word, which reveals His character, His heart, and His desire for us. And if that wasn't enough, He gave us Jesus, the word became flesh and dwelt among us, so that we could look fully into the face of God and know Him intimately. Shut the front door!

The day I fled from God because of truth deprivation and truth poisoning was the day I ran straight into the arms of a life of desolation, meaninglessness, and hopelessness. At age seventeen, I married my troublemaking boyfriend in jail. We had only been married a few months when he went to prison for assault on a police officer. A few days after he left, I discovered that I was a few weeks pregnant with our first child, a boy. When my husband was finally released on parole our son was a little over three years old. Throughout the next seven years, we traveled all over Texas because my husband made a living in the oil fields. Although my husband had always liked his beer, his drinking intensified as did his craving to be with more women than I could shake a stick at. It was not uncommon for him to take a short run to the store for a pack of cigarettes only to return two to three weeks later.

There are stories about his unfaithfulness that I just can't share for fear of wounding women in my life that I should have been able to trust, so I won't. Truth-be-told it wouldn't change a thing! I was around the age of 21 when we had our daughter and our last child. It was when I was around the age of 24 that one evening my husband came home from an AA meeting, commode-hugging, and knee-walking drunk. When I grasped how drunk he was I made the unintentional blunder of asking him if he was tanked-up again, which sent him over the edge to the point of him yelling and throwing furniture. When He came at me in a fit of drunken rage, with his fist held high and intent on using me as his punching bag I managed to duck, which caused his hand to collide with the mirror behind me. Even though his hand was in sore shape, and he had to be in a world of pain, he was hell-bent on hurting me and I was not fast enough to escape him when he lunged for me. I can still hear my children, who were about 4 and 7, terrified and crying and they begged, "Daddy stop! Daddy, please! Stop!"

Although we had many altercations when he was under the influence there was only one other time that I could recollect being truly scared out of my wits and that was when he had snatched all the wires out from under the hood of my car to keep me from leaving the house.

With blood trickling off the gashes of his hand, he took hold of my arms, threw me on the bed, wrapped his strong, calloused hands around my neck, and began to squeeze my throat. I couldn't breathe and tears were flowing out of my eyes as I watched my traumatized babies huddling together in a corner, scared to death and yelling for their daddy to stop! If I close my eyes and think on it now, I can still see my baby boy holding his small sister in such a way as to protect her if the time came. The thought that this would be the last thing my babies' little eyes would see and that if my husband was successful, they would be next in line petrified me more than dying itself. I truly believe that in that moment my Heavenly Father intervened because I was able, amidst the fear and the intense weight of his body and increasing pressure of his hands around my neck, to squeak out the words, "Look at the children."

Of all the words to come out of my mouth, you would have thought it would be stop. I truly believe it was God fighting on my behalf because amid his rage and drunkenness, there was a split second, which felt so much longer, where my husband paused and turned his head toward the screaming and frightened faces of our sweet babies. In that moment a look of something I can't even begin to describe washed over him and his grip relaxed on my neck, just enough for me to push him into the broken mirror, grab my babies, and run for our lives. It was about two or three years later that our divorce was final. Several years further down the road I received a call that he had been killed in an accident while driving drunk. The man in the car with him at the time survived but the 18-year-old boy in the car he hit did not. It breaks my heart!

A few months before my divorce was final, I met my soon-to-be husband, Bob. I had never had anyone make such a fuss over me the way he did and still does. I realized many, many years ago that when I married my Robert, I probably didn't love him as much as I loved the way he treated me. Now we joke about the fact that I also thought he was rich because he drove a Subaru and all its doors opened, and it didn't need to be started with a coke bottle hitting the battery or gas being poured into the carburetor. Truth-be-told I also think that I was in love with the idea of escaping Texas and what I considered to be a life of hell.

Any hoot, Robert and I met in October, he proposed in January, and then in March, one month after my divorce was final, we got married. At the time we were hitched he was in the Air Force, so the kids and I got our green cards and fled the grand ol' country of Texas to set up residence in the foreign land of New Jersey. You have no idea how true those words are for it was like being in another country for this Texas girl. Within a couple of years, I secured a job with a music distributor and reveled in the awards I won for a job well done. A few years into our marriage my husband adopted both our children and has never ever treated them otherwise. He is a man after my own heart, my knight-in-shining-armor. I love him more than words can express and more than I ever thought possible.

So yes, I finally had everything I had always dreamed of and wanted. I had everything that I thought I needed to make me whole and happy! A great husband, two beautiful kids, an awesome job, a home with food on the table, clothes on our back, security, and so much more. Yet, even then, I felt like something was wrong, something was missing. After my honey retired from the military we decided to settle down in

Pennsylvania where we ultimately bought our first home. My fairy tale life had come true and happily ever after was a sure thing. That is until the day my dreams began to shatter one by one and the things that I thought held me together and made me important and valuable were nothing but dung.

We began to have problems—that's an understatement—with our teenage daughter, and life was once again not what I had hoped or dreamed it would be. I won't get into all the details, but the turmoil that took place in our house had made me plumb bone weary, and the situation in our home was almost to the point of being unbearable. Things had escalated so beyond what I thought I could take that one day while driving home from work, I began to look for a cliff to drive off.

Late at night, while everyone was sleeping, I would go into our bathroom, sit on the floor, and weep uncontrollably, sometimes with my hand over my mouth so that no one could hear my wailing. I just wanted to die! It just so happened that one night as I was going about my routine of weeping and wailing while lying on the bathroom floor, I began to cry out for God to help me! I can't even begin to explain it, but it was so clear to me that God was there and that He was impressing upon my heart to get a Bible. Now mind you finding a Bible in our house was a miracle, but God is in the business of miracles. I finally found an old Bible of my husband's that he had gotten when he was in Catholic school. Not knowing what to look for or where to look I randomly opened the big Bible laced with pictures, and began to read the following . . .

Isaiah 58:8-14 (NKJV) —
"Then your light shall break forth like the morning,
Your healing shall spring forth speedily,
And your righteousness shall go before you;
The glory of the LORD shall be your rear guard.
Then you shall call, and the LORD will answer;
You shall cry, and He will say, 'Here I am.'

"If you take away the yoke from your midst,
The pointing of the finger, and speaking wickedness,

If you extend your soul to the hungry
And satisfy the afflicted soul,
Then your light shall dawn in the darkness,
And your darkness shall be as the noonday.
The LORD *will guide you continually,*
And satisfy your soul in drought,
And strengthen your bones;
You shall be like a watered garden,
And like a spring of water, whose waters do not fail.
Those from among you
Shall build the old waste places;
You shall raise up the foundations of many generations;
And you shall be called the Repairer of the Breach,
The Restorer of Streets to Dwell In.

"If you turn away your foot from the Sabbath,
From doing your pleasure on My holy day,
And call the Sabbath a delight,
The holy day of the LORD *honorable,*
And shall honor Him, not doing your own ways,
Nor finding your own pleasure,
Nor speaking your own words,
Then you shall delight yourself in the LORD*;*
And I will cause you to ride on the high hills of the earth,
And feed you with the heritage of Jacob your father.
The mouth of the LORD *has spoken."*

So right there, while I was spread out on the bathroom floor like an old used-up and dirty rag, searching for truth and hope like my life depended on it, and it did, my all-knowing and loving God reached down. In my limited exposure to His word, ignorance of the knowledge of God, and lack of grasping the word of God, I sensed that God was telling me that if I would turn to Him and go to church, he would make it all better. So, I determined in my heart that very night, that come hell or high water, I was going to church the next Sunday. That night I crawled into bed and slept like a baby in its mama's womb, and I hadn't slept like that in a good long while.

That following Sunday, I was so excited I could spit as I vaulted out of bed and commenced getting ready to go to church. I think my husband had the notion that I had gone off the deep end, but he wasn't about to step in and try to stop me. I told you he is not only the best but also very smart! Any hoot, I began to look up churches in our area in the phone directory, ultimately settling upon one particular church all because the person who answered the phone that Sunday morning, was kind, inviting, patient with my questions, and had a southern accent to boot. God is good! He knew I'd need to hear His words in my own language! I must say I was as nervous as fly in a flyswatter factory, since the last time I had been to church was over twenty years before and we all know how well that turned out.

Well, I did what most new people do when they first visit an unfamiliar church. I snuck in as quietly as possible, trying not to be noticed by anyone, and planted myself in the back row. It makes my belly laugh when I think about it because it was such a welcoming church that I think I could have been sitting on the roof and they would have managed to find me. It still blows my mind, stirs up my heart, and makes my eyes leak when I think about how much God revealed His love for me on that day. There was not one part of the service, from the worship, the message, to the invitation that was not truth-filled and aimed at my brokenness and need. The pastor began to preach on Galatians 2:20. The words wrapped around my heart like a vise grip and began to squeeze tears out of my eyes. Galatians 2:20 became the first verse that I collected in my heart because God made sure to declare it over and over again that day, through song and word. Wowsa! Forgive my expounding upon His precious truth . . . But this is what I wrestled with in my heart as He pursued me through His words.

Galatians 2:20 — *"I (The one who is invisible, worthless, alone, damaged merchandise and who has lost all hope and just wants to die)* **am crucified with Christ**. *(You gave your all for me even when I ran away from you, turned my back on you! Can I live my life for you?)* **and yet I live** *(Amazing* *grace and love, for now, I see that you have never let me go. You have pursued, protected, and called me even when I was content to live my life apart from you. I broke your heart).* **Not I,** *(I am not alone in this!)* **but Christ lives in me** *(It is more than I can understand!)* **and the life I now live** *(Standing on His promises, filled with His presence, no longer hopeless.)* **I live by faith** *(I can trust Him. He is not like those that have broken my heart. He is trustworthy and more than able)* **in the Son of God** *(My Jesus, my Savior, my King)* **who loved me** *(Even when no one else did and when He had no reason to)* **and gave Himself** *(Everything)* **for me.** *(He loves me like no other!)"*

The truth met me head-on and so profoundly that I was in tears and my body shook from the gamut of emotions God's word roused in me. I finally understood that all my life I had been attempting to fill the God-sized hole in my life with everything but Him. And although my heart was on its knees in surrender fear kept me frozen in my seat.

Oh, if we only recognized and got just how much He loves us! His love is so evident. Even as I write this, I can't help but cry, smile, and praise Him. For even when fear held me in my seat He continued to reach deep down into the pit of my fear and brokenness, by not only speaking to me through His word being read and preached but by serving up His truth and expressing His love for me through a young man who sang a song called "I Am Crucified with Christ" by Phillips Craig and Dean. I encourage you to take a moment sometime, sit for a spell and soak in the words of this beautiful song.

As the words of the song unfolded and my tears ran freely, my fingers began to loosen their grip on the pew in front of me and when the pastor invited anyone ready to place their life in the hands of God and take them out of the hands of an idiot (not his words), I walked down that aisle, knelt at the altar and gave my life over, lock, stock and barrel, to the One who has loved me with His all. Ain't nobody ever loved me like my Jesus and there is no other name by which we can be saved. I am so thankful for God's mercy and His relentless love.

In **Isaiah 58**, the scripture I went to that night in the bathroom, He says: *"you shall call, and the LORD will answer; You shall cry, and He will say, 'Here I am.'* I sought the Lord and He answered me!

He is so faithful and trustworthy!

You know I went home that day from church a much different woman than when I first walked through its doors. I do have to admit that when I got home that day, I stood at our front door and paused for a moment as I wondered if things at home had improved. They had not! But although circumstances in our home had not changed God indeed had changed me in my circumstances.

I spent so much time, too much time, wallowing in the lies of a fallen and broken world when all along I could have been living in the light of His truth and love. It makes my eyes leak when I think about all that time I spent dancing in the hog trough, content with the taste and the stench of slop when I could have been soaring on the wings of His truth and grace. So much time was spent in a man-made prison due to lack of truth, when right before my eyes was the King of Kings, the Lord of Lords holding out the key to my freedom.

It has been the truth of God's word that has set me free from the bondage, the shackles of my past, feelings, circumstances, and other's opinions as well as the lies and twisted truths that old deceiver Satan has spewed forth. It has been the truth of God's love, His character, His promises, and His will for my life that has moved me from grazing on astroturf to strolling in green pastures. I spent twenty years dancing in the hog trough, believing the lies of Satan, and living my life apart from the One and only One who could, would, and has fought for me. That's a bitter pill to swallow!

Yep, I confess that I had the runs for a good portion of my life. But that's what happens when you go dancing in the hog trough, content to eat and live off the slop of lies slung at you throughout your life instead of turning the question around on that old deceiver Satan by going to the word of God to seek the answers to the question the devil so often throws at us, "But did God really say?"

God's word says there is a way that seems right to man (bless our hearts) but in the end, it leads to death! You know I've realized that the devil is more than willing and very capable of making the hog trough of his rotten, tough-as-stewed skunk and putrid lies look non-toxic, appetizing, sweeter than stolen honey, and risk-free to boot, just like my ex-lax cake. I can explain it to you, but I can't make you understand it.

But trust me, cross my heart, and hope to spit, truth-poisoning will not only give you the runs, make you sore as a boil, and cause your heart to be cold as a cast-iron commode but it will make you as full of pains as an old window. Shucks it will make sliding down an eight-foot razor blade and landing in a bowl of alcohol look like a day at the beach! And if that ain't bad enough, you can bet the farm that you will find yourself running from and not in the direction of the only One who can save, heal, and set you free from the intense hunger pains of dancing in the hog trough and living on the devil's slop of lies.

So next time the devil strikes and whispers in your ear, "But did God really say?" kick him where it hurts with the word of God! Go to your Abba Daddy, feast on His word, and see that the Lord is good! Just say no to dancing in the hog trough! Pigs get fat but hogs, well pardon my Texanese, they get slaughtered. That's all she wrote!

Disclaimer: I have nothing against hogs, but I do have an aversion to being slaughtered!

C. S. Lewis said, "If you look for truth, you will find comfort in the end. If you look for comfort you will not get either comfort or truth, only soft soap and wishful thinking to begin, and in the end, despair."

Church is out! Or is it?

CHAPTER FOUR

SHUT THE DOOR! YOU WEREN'T BORN IN A BARN!

On the beautiful, joyful, monumental, and life-transforming Sunday morning when I surrendered my heart, soul, mind, and oomph to my Savior I was schooled on two things: following Christ does not always alter our state-of-affairs and Christ is more than able, if we depend on Him, to change our outlook and our uptake in the circumstances that may not change! Now, I do suppose there may be a good number of folks, ignorant or otherwise, who may have misinterpreted, misunderstood, or twisted the truth out of character, in that they presume that life as a follower of Christ is as easy as a Sunday evening drive or a leisurely walk through a beautiful garden. Well, I don't know about you but where I come from, no matter how beautiful or tranquil a garden on this earth may be, roses still have thorns, flowers grow alongside weeds, and both threatening and harmless-looking critters still scurry back and forth seeking to gobble up the good things.

I ain't just whistling Dixie when I say that we just might be naïve or ignorant if we believe that we can just shove our fingers in our ears, place our hands over our eyes, and reject the notion that without tending and safeguarding our gardens they will struggle, wither, and possibly perish. And heavens to Betsy if that ain't enough to get our undies in a bunch, it is the God's honest truth that over yonder and beyond the tall and protective fencing surrounding our garden are ravenous and destructive vermin prowling about, nipping at the bit, drooling at the mouth, and eyeballing for a way inside to devour the hearty things blossoming. But, for fear that we be unmindful and hence give the wrong impression, we need to be alerted to the truth that some of those critters may even now have managed to climb over, burrow an opening under or chomp their way through our fence. And if we reckon they don't have the gumption or wherewithal to scramble over a fence then I've got an ocean in the Sahara Desert I'd like to sell you. Well, butter my backside and call me a biscuit, you should see the plucky, mammoth-sized, full as a tick on a dog, and obviously skillful groundhog that makes no bones about scrambling over our neighbor's fence to get into their vegetable garden.

I'll tell you what, sometimes these pillagers don't even have to muster up the effort to climb over the fence. Oftentimes, we've rolled out the welcome mat to the devasting little parasites by just plumb leaving our garden gate door swung wide open for them to parade on in and ramble about the shadowy nooks and crannies of our garden, seemingly undetected because they have mastered the art of being quieter than a mouse peeing on cotton. No matter how these rascally pests were able to make inroads into our garden it's essential that we recognize and grasp the notion that they are proficient at camouflaging themselves very well. They will seek out the most unnoticed and unattended section in our garden and camp out there. And if we don't give them the boot, they will sooner or later get too big for their britches, grow fat and sassy as they scarf down whatever don't or won't eat them first. I'm not even sure how we manage to take no notice of them when honest-to-Pete; they are, roughly speaking, about as foul-smelling as an outhouse breeze.

Before we start blaming our lack of fruit-bearing and our garden wasteland on these insatiable creatures and targeting fault on that fiendish, slithering, lying Satan we may perhaps need to put some thought to it. Yes indeedy, that mean-filled, cunning, foul-mouth, sneaky, deceiving, lie-breathing devil is roaming the earth looking for someone to devour, but we don't have to roll out the red carpet, lay out the welcome mat, answer the door when he comes ringing our bell, and provide him with an all-you-can-eat buffet. Hoot there it is! I remember as a kid watching a show called Flip Wilson, where the go-to line for the main character, Geraldine, when she did something immoral, was to point the finger and excuse her bad behavior by exclaiming, "The devil made me do it"!

Y'all, I think sometimes we just give Satan way too much credit! He has no power over us other than what we give him. Ain't that the truth. We, as Holy Spirit filled Christians, can decide to take up the welcome mat today and shut the door to his deceiving and harmful schemes!

Anyone who is genuinely familiar with me is also acquainted with the amusing fact that I am apt to wrestle with yielding sweet-smelling flowers or tasty vegetables in my garden of weedin'. So, for me to school someone about the essentials of gardening is like burning daylight! No police line-up is necessary, for the list of crimes against any sort of vegetation is long and I will be the first to fess up and reveal that I am guilty as the day is long! My crimes include death by asphyxiation for a good many defenseless cactuses while living in Las Vegas, attempted homicide by waterboarding a harmless man-made plant, and verbal assault of countless innocent blossoms that just didn't have a snowball's chance in Texas of survival because I yakked them into an early grave.

Shucks, I have a noble friend who took such pity upon my lack of a green thumb that she passed onto me a couple of her thriving baby's breath to plant because she was convinced, beyond a shadow of a doubt, that they were impervious to being massacred. Later, not that much later I might add, it devastated my heart when I had to go to her, head down and shamefaced, and own up to the fact that her ever-lasting baby's breath that she had so thoughtfully placed in my care had bit the dust, bought the farm, kicked the bucket, and ceased breathing! Just sayin.' And let me tell you, when it comes to weeding, well goodness gracious me, don't you know I'm a might put out, because I tussle with the challenge of knowing which vegetation to yank or to hang onto because sometimes the weeds in my garden look more animated and smell more fragrant than the flowers. Yep, when it comes to horticulture, I am as lost as last year's Easter egg. No might could about it! You've been forewarned!

One precious night I had a couple of mighty loveable, sweet ladies over for a bible study at my home and even though I was so thrilled I could spit to share with them some ground-breaking news, I held my britches and my horses as I sensed the need to wait till we were wrapping up our study for the night to spill the sensational news flash.

"Ladies, guess what I got today!"

Their expressions showed anticipation and delight as they quickly asked, "What?"

"I got Chlamydia!"

Of course, I was so jam-packed with enthusiasm and raring to share with them my unbelievable newsflash that it never, not once ever, crossed my pea-picking great brain or struck me wrong that the look on their faces when I made my extraordinary declaration was more that of dumbfounded shock than of awestricken amazement.

One of the more considerate and genteel ladies of the group, bent forward and with a soft hushed voice and a slightly blushed face inquired of me, "Where did you get IT?"

Completely oblivious to her feeling the need to speak in a very low voice, I couldn't help but boldly and proudly declare with ignorant satisfaction and button-popping pride just oozing from my Texas pores, "At Lowes!"

It still cracks me up when I think about the look of distress and bewilderment on their overly concerned faces. Oh, but there are no words in my massive Texanese dictionary that could ever, thoroughly, or accurately represent the countenance on their unsuspecting faces when I said with more insistence than invitation, "Y'all gotta come and see my Chlamydia!"

Again, I would like to state on my behalf that I was just so pants-dancing pleased and enveloped in my mind-blowing gardening triumph that I didn't even give a second thought to cross-examining them about their uncharacteristic, peculiar reactions to my joyful revelation or their lack of curious anticipation, as I elbowed and implored them to come and take a looksee. Like cows being led to the stockyard, I wrangled those pleasant, yet apprehensive ladies right out my front door and with a smile of gratification broadcasted my news to anyone within earshot of hearing, "Isn't my Chlamydia beautiful?"

If I'd felt any better, I would have thought it was a setup! Their look of heartfelt relief for my newly honed gardening skills that had produced such good-looking Chlamydia made my pants want to get up and dance and my face grin. However, what I could not comprehend nor wrap my head around (which houses a big brain, trust me I have pictures) was their odd reactions! Don't you know I was even more confused when those sweet, wouldn't-harm-a-fly ladies broke out into fits of bent-over, tears-down-your-legs all out laughter. Once they could suck in oxygen again, they tenderly and graciously, with many a few giggles here and there, made clear the reason for their relief and their all-out laughing fit. So, that day I was schooled in the reality that the eye-pleasing flowers that I had so painstakingly planted, watered, and observed bloom, which was so rare for me to experience, were not Chlamydia but Clematis. Another new word for my expanding dictionary! The struggle is real, y'all! Trust me!

When I handed over my life to Christ one beautiful Sunday morning it was not the completion of my journey but just the beginning. Unbeknownst to me there was a whole lot of weeding, pruning, tilling, fertilizing, and pest control necessary in my garden, and there still is, to enable me to live my life, sold out and fruitful for Him. What I've learned about my Lord, who is the Master Gardener, is that He doesn't cotton to nor adhere to the old saying, "I'm fixin' to commence to begin to get ready to start." From the moment we are willing and able and say, "I Do," He begins a good work in us. Thank the good Lord that He is faithful to complete it!

Good gravy, don't you know, wasn't it that very same Sunday night that my ever-loving, all-knowing, and long-suffering God, who has mind-boggling timing as well as an immense sense of humor, chose to get about His business and commence some pruning and cultivating in my garden. Just as I was tiptoeing past my used-to-be delightful, turned demon-seed baby girl's room God began yanking at the weeds and pouncing on the damaging critters bedding down in the shady alcoves of the garden of my heart and I didn't like it one iota. Anyone who had been a fly on the wall that evening would have dropped their jaw and dribbled a bit as they eavesdropped on the tete-a-tete, or should I say tug of war, going on between me and my Abba Daddy right there in the hallway in front of the demon seed's shut bedroom door. Truth-be-told, all that God was requesting of me was to say three little words, "I love you" to a rebellious teenager that I no longer recognized and most certainly did not like!

Yep, there I was, brand-spanking fresh off the printing presses of yielding my life to Christ, a newborn babe in the woods, my garden a hot mess, and my Heavenly Father was squandering no time at all by challenging the weeds of anger, bitterness, and resentment that I was cleaving to. If you have ever tried to take a pacifier away from a baby, then you have an idea of the oh-no-you-don't conflict warring in me when God said, "Let it go!"

So, for several minutes, that seemed more like an eternity, God and I went back and forth, forth and back about whether or not I should surrender my comfort food of harmful and debilitating feelings that I was tightly clutching to my chest and mosey on into our little hellion's room where I knew I was in jeopardy of getting scorched by her outraged eyes or worse yet, devoured by her inconsiderate words and attitude. Now don't get me wrong, God wasn't asking any more of me than He isn't more than capable of delivering but in that split-second, my want-to was fading and my get-up-and-go had gotten up and left. I guess you could say I had a hitch in my git-along! Yes, I admit I had a stinking-thinking problem, and trust me God got a whiff of its stench long before I positioned my heart, my very existence at the foot of His all-knowing, wise, and holy presence.

Well, I scrapped with the Lord and the Lord won! I reluctantly staggered, dragging my feet as much as I could get away with, into our daughter's chamber of horrors, full well expecting to be a casualty of a head-on collision with the leading character from *The Exorcist*, only to unearth the realization and truth that God's fruit-producing powers are so much better than mine and that He really does have this gardening stuff down. He knows what He is doing! Ain't that a hoot? The experience validated the declaration once again that when I placed my hands in His ever-capable hands I most certainly did take it out of the hands of an idiot!

It's funny—not funny ha-ha—that all God compelled of me that night was utter to my rebellious girl that I loved her. That's it! Who would have thunk that those three words, "I love you", would be so hard-hitting and exhausting, and that by heeding His voice and not giving full audience to my fears that lurked in the garden of my mind and enflamed my heart, it could or would kick off a transformation. And what a change it was! Oh, not so much in my daughter! She was still a demon seed! But in me! Although I do have to say there was a split-second moment when it seemed like her head stopped revolving and pea soup ceased to spew out of her mouth! I'm sorry! But who would have thunk it!

I reckon, right now before God and you, I will pinky-swear to the fact and admit that I can be so thick-headed that you could smack me in the face with a tire iron and I won't yell till morning. In truth, our life with our girl didn't get better, in fact, it got worse. But after we rode out and lived through the storm of her rebelliousness and drug addiction, only by my Abba Daddy's grace and strength, she came to me and spoke words I never imagined hearing. "Mom, with everything I put you through and everything that has happened there was never a time when I didn't know that you loved me." Still makes my eyes leak, y'all.

Ecclesiastes 7:9 (NIV) — *"Do not be quickly provoked in your spirit, for anger resides in the lap of fools."*

Yep, if we are gonna hold on to those nasty pests; bitterness, resentment, and anger, we might as well change our name to fool because that is exactly what we act like! Been there! Done that! Guilty as charged!

When our kids were toddlers, we lived in a little two-room (not counting the bathroom) country shack located far out in the boondocks of Texas that I'm fairly sure was held up only by twigs, tumbleweeds, and a prayer. Although the little shanty wasn't much to shake a stick at, we did have a pot to pee in and a window to throw it out of, so by poor-folk criteria we were walking in high cotton compared to some folks. When we first moved into our unassuming abode, we took notice of an unfamiliar but faint humming sound but chalked the odd melody up to the house being older than dirt and dreadfully well-ventilated. Several days after moving in I became well aware that not only had the humming racket become more like a buzzing which had intensified, but that the peculiar disturbance was now coming from every wall in the house. Well curiosity killed the cat, no news is good news and what you don't know won't hurt you, so I chose to pay no never mind to our vibrating and buzzing walls! That is, until the day I was startled awake by not one, two, three, or four bees buzzing about mine and the kids' heads, but hordes of them. How we got out of there with only one person getting stung beats me, but it turned out that every wall in our shack was infested and bursting to the brim with bees, glorious bees. Ain't that a hoot!

Ezekiel 36:26 (ESV) — *"And I will give you a new heart, and a new spirit I will put within you. And I will remove the heart of stone from your flesh and give you a heart of flesh."*

On the day I placed my life in the hands of my ever-loving Savior, God in His love and grace fixed His holy eyes upon the dirty, unkempt, unfruitful garden of my heart, crowded with life-sucking scroungers and a plethora of foul-smelling weeds and began to clear the land, prune the branches, and till the soil. Things in my past; abandonment, abuse, rejection, and sinful choices had turned out an overabundance of oxygen-sucking, nauseating, death-inducing fruit-destroying pests in my garden. And just like the bees in the wall of our rickety little lean-to, which I had grown so accustomed to their everyday assault on my senses that I was able to ignore and live with it, I realized that I had also acclimated myself so well to the putrid stench of the weeds and vermin of my past that I had become desensitized to the stinking thinking that continually and relentlessly assaulted my mind and heart.

2 Corinthians 5:17 (NET) — *"So then, if anyone is in Christ, he is a new creation; what is old has passed away—look, what is new has come!"*

My mama got hitched at the suitable old marrying age of twelve to my biological father who at the time of their betrothal was at the advanced old age of twenty-six years. One day, when my mom was fourteen years young, she was defrosting the refrigerator when without warning or expectation she started to have excruciating back and abdominal pains. My mom's relentless agony terrified her so much that she instantaneously assumed she was knocking on heaven's door and began to scream for help. My father, not knowing what was really going on, obliged her wishes by calling for an ambulance. I can still recall my mother's giggle and picture her eyes lighting up as she recounted the tale of her first child's (that's me) delivery. As the ambulance quickly fled through the quiet streets of Austin, she swore her screams were so loud that everyone could hear her wild squealing echoing into the pitch-black Texas night.

She was so distressed by the unexpected onslaught and the sudden severe painful sensations that she began to plead with the ambulance attendants to get her to the hospital before she croaked. It was then, that young ambulance attendant calmly hollered out, over her screams of misery and woe, "Honey you ain't dying, you're having a baby!"

It still makes me grin from ear to ear and chuckle inside and out when I think about her child-bride innocence as she in her deer-in-the-headlight disbelief snapped and countered the attendant's courageous and unexpected statement with, "I'm having a WHAT?"

Yep, it's a fact, that my mother went nine months with me growing in her belly without any inkling at all that a little redheaded girl was stewing in her womb, eager and ready to invade her world and shake it up mightily. Many years down the road a spell, as my mother told me about my birthing day, she shared that it was as the ambulance attendant revealed the update of my impending birth, that she just happened to glance out of the ambulance window and spot the Capital building all decked out finer than frog fur, with more flags than you could shake a stick at. In fact, she was astounded and plumb-tickled that there were flags soaring and waving everywhere she gawked. Honest-to-Pete, I reckon it wasn't till I was perhaps in my late twenties before I learned that June 14, Flag Day was not all about me. Ain't that a hoot! I was born at night, but not last night y'all! Yep, I'm not stupid, I'm just ignorant!

Well, my mother endeavored to do the best she could with what she knew about mothering. I'm not making excuses for her waywardness, for I would have crossed my heart and hoped to die sworn that excuses would or could not ever escape my mouth. I wish I could have grasped some of these necessary insights when I was younger, but what's done is done. It makes me sad when I think upon the many times, I would throw rocks at my mama and call her horrendous names that a child shouldn't have known anything about. Albeit my grandmother would work me into a fit of brokenhearted fury by telling me appalling junk about my mother's behaviors and activities (mostly true), followed up by a huge helping of how my mother didn't love or want me. I'm not making excuses for my dishonorable behavior, but I will and can say that I was just a child who looked around at the sad state of affairs I was in, and the goings-on of my mother and determined every foul and malicious thing spilling out of my grandmother's mouth was the truth. Only God knows the whole truth, so I'll leave that at the cross!

Any hoot, after six weeks of catering to a newborn baby, and a red-headed girl to boot, my mother just couldn't take it, nor me anymore, and so I was handed over to the management of my grandmother (mama) and grandfather (papa). Later in life, I joked at a women's conference I was speaking at that my mother was the one who devised disposable diapers. The story was that every time my mom had to change a diaper (they were cloth then) instead of dealing with the soiled mess, which made her gag, she would throw the stinky garment over their fence and into the neighbor's yard. Disposable diapers! I warned you that anything can come flying over that fence, didn't I!

Well, way down the road of my ventures with my mother she expressed grief for passing me over to my grandmother, and she pondered upon what she must have been thinking for she was all too familiar with what my life would be like under my grandmother's watchful strict supervision. It never occurred to me till it was much too late, that my mother must have had a pretty tough childhood as well—at least what little of it there was. I did get to see my mother and my other siblings off and on throughout my young life when she would come to visit her mother, my grandmother. My mom had three more children by the time she was seventeen or eighteen. Two she kept, a boy and a girl, and another girl that we never met because she was given up for adoption. I think my mother was looking for love in all the wrong places. The garden of her heart had to be infested with many nasty vermin—been there, done that—for she married several times and had many lovers and affairs.

I think over time I grew very bitter over the realization that my mother gave me away and kept my other siblings. I resented the fact that she left me with my harsh grandmother and that my mom seemed not to care about what may or may not be happening to me. I resented that as kids and young adults we had to call our mom by her given name, and we were not allowed to call her mom because she didn't want others to know she had birthed babies. But mostly, I hated her (I know that sounds harsh) for the fear I had every night when I had to lie in the same bed next to my grandmother. I hated that I was concerned about her opinion of me or her attitude and actions toward me. I hated that I not only loved her but that I needed and ached for her love and approval so very desperately.

Even though my mother didn't raise me it never changed the fact that she was my mother and that I longed very much to have a genuine mother-daughter relationship with her. I held a lot of resentment toward her for not keeping me and for so many other things as well. It wasn't until I was thirty-seven, when I had handed over my life to Christ that I became mindful of the truth that I needed to change how I responded and reacted in my relationship with my mother, whether she did or not.

The second that thought truly sunk in, fear the size of Texas washed over me, and I have to admit that acting upon that realization and conviction scared me half to death. I reckon to me it was about the same as asking someone covered in fresh blood to dive into shark-infested waters without the expectation of getting eaten alive or asking me to jump into water when I can't swim a lick. It's silly when I think on it but not forgiving my mom was the only thing that gave me some sense of control and power over her and my life. Or at least that's what I thought! It's ironic that holding on to all the hurt, anger and pain really didn't give me diddly-squat, in fact it accomplished precisely the opposite. Now mind you, my mother never asked for forgiveness but that didn't alter the fact that I needed to and should pardon her. I am so appreciative that God changed me from the inside out by pulling those weeds of unforgiveness, resentment, anger, bitterness, and fear and planted beautiful flowers in my heart of compassion, empathy, and love for my mom that far exceeded what I could ever imagine possible. He is so much better at gardening than I am. Thank you, Lord!

It sticks in my throat like hair on a biscuit when I consider how we waste so much of this life bearing grudges and holding back forgiveness from those who have hurt us. I remember hearing someone proclaim that they had forgiven someone 490 times and that biblically (Matthew 18:22) they were okay and did not have to forgive them anymore.

Matthew 18:22 where Peter says, *"Lord, how many times shall I forgive someone who sins against me? Up to seven times?' Jesus responded, "I tell you, not seven times, but seventy times seven."*

A few of us may be guilty when we read this, of going straightway to our fingers, toes, or our calculator and tallying it all up. Whew, we just might think 490 times is all we have to forgive someone and that we are finished. No more! We can give the hurt mongers a Texas-size boot to the curb while we take pleasure in wallowing in our anger and resentment, and feel we are well within our rights to boot! Believe it or not, but we may have missed the entire point.

Genesis 4:24 — The song of Lamech. Lamech was a descendant of Cain who had inherited Cain's homicidal instinct, but actually ended up outdoing even Cain.
"I have killed a man for wounding me,
A young man for injuring me.
If Cain is avenged seven times,
Then Lamech seventy-seven times (seventy times seven)."

Honest-to-Pete, if you got on the wrong bad side of Lamech he would have settled up with you big time, not just seven times, but seventy times seven. In God's word seven is a number that represents completeness. But get this, for Lamech, his revenge or avenging ways didn't just come to a halt with seven but went way outside done and over with. Goodness me, Lamech would make a hornet look cuddly! His garden was infested with vermin as bitterness, anger, and resentment ran rampant.

I think Jesus is saying to all of us, that is, His followers, that we should be as enthusiastic to forgive as Lamech was as zealous to take his revenge. That's a tough thought to swallow for sure! Lamech avowed to punish others way beyond the injury or wrongdoing that was carried out against him. But Jesus . . . says we should be the reverse of Lamech and make it our aim to forgive to the moon and back, and beyond. That's heavy!

Y'all forgiveness does not mean that what is done to you is acceptable or okie dokie; that you will comprehend the why or what of it all; that someone will not have to face the consequences or penalties of decisions made; that relationships are always reconciled; that there will be no fear of getting hurt again; that you will forget or that you will ever trust that person in the same way again. Forgiveness just means you let go of the back-breaking, energy-draining, weed-inducing burden of taking on the responsibility to be the wrongdoers judge, jury, and executioner and place it where it belongs, in the nail-pierced hands of a holy, loving, faithful, righteous, and just God who sings over you; fights for you; walks with you; heals the brokenhearted; holds your tears in a bottle and will one day bring everything to light, even the motives of your heart and mine. Guess this is the place where we all just might need to collapse before Him and ask for forgiveness because I know the motives of my heart are not always the will of His. Father, forgive us for we know not what we do, and Father help us to forgive others for that very same reason!

Psalm 27:13-14 (NLT) —
> *"Yet I am confident I will see the LORD's goodness*
> *while I am here in the land of the living.*
> *Wait patiently for the LORD.*
> *Be brave and courageous.*
> *Yes, wait patiently for the LORD."*

A couple of years down the road of my wild adventure with my Jesus, my mom gave me a holler to ask me how I; the one she did not keep, the one she did not raise, the one she had hurt so much, could love her and forgive her after all her wrongdoings. I could only speak the truth,

"Mama, how could I not forgive you when I have been forgiven so much, so extravagantly, so completely by my Lord and Savior!"

My mom was silent. Up to that point, I don't think I had ever told my mama I had forgiven her, but I guess my actions spoke louder than words. My mama then told me she was sorry and that she loved me and mourned over the things she had done.

A couple of months later, she called on a Sunday afternoon to tell me that she had gone to church that morning and fallen into the loving and merciful arms of Jesus our Savior. Praiseallujah! My mama never asked for my forgiveness, and I'd be untruthful with you if I said that she never did or said anything else to wound me. But I'd also be two-faced if I said I never did or said anything to break her heart. All I can say is that I made a choice, prompted by the loving nudging of my Abba Daddy living in the garden of my heart, and it was in His strength and by His power, and not mine, that I was able to forgive and love my mama like my Jesus has loved and forgiven me. Truth-be-told I fell short many a time when it came to loving my mama like Jesus loves me.

I remember the day my mama died like it was only yesterday, December 26th, 2013. On December 23rd, I received THE call. It was my sisters' tearful voice calling to tell me that the doctors were not giving my mama much time to live—a few days at the most. After I hung up the phone I fell to my knees and cried out and wept for my mama and if I'm being honest, I wept for me, in such a way that I would have never—nay ever—thought likely. I then called up my mama and spoke with her for as long as she could maintain a conversation, as she was weak and at times a little incoherent. I struggled to make the arrangements to get to Texas to see my Mama before the good Lord took her home, but an impending snowstorm was threatening and impeding my plans. On December 24th, 2013, my mama startled me by calling in the early morning hours to wish me a Merry Christmas. She was coherent but weak, and we had but only few minutes before her voice trailed off in which I was able to tell her once again that I loved her and to soak in the sweet words I loved to hear from my mama's lips, "I love you more".

After that, my mama was no longer able to carry on a conversation. On December 26th, I began to write about my mama and God's amazing faithfulness in giving me peace and more love and compassion for her than I ever thought imaginable. My heart gushed out onto the pages before me and it was as I was bringing the saga of my journey with my mama to its closing stages that the next words startlingly trickled out onto the pages, "Today my mama is walking into the presence of Jesus." God rocked my world, for no sooner had the words cascaded onto the pages than my phone began to ring. It was my brother, knee-deep in sorrow, calling to say that our mama was absent from the body but present with the Lord!

On December 26th, my mama, who I loved with all my transformed and redeemed heart, was restored to health, and received into the arms of our loving Savior. As I stood on my back porch that morning, alone and sobbing for the loss of my mama God sprinkled down the most beautiful pure-white snowflakes this Texas girl has ever seen. I could feel His magnificent presence all around me and I found comfort and peace in the arms of His love and the truth that He loves me so much He will never take His eyes off me.

I never thought I would one day say these words . . . but I miss my mama's presence in my life now. I have surprised myself many times over the past few years when I've reached to pick up the phone to call my mama . . . only to become aware that this temporary, whack-a-doodle, decomposing world is no longer her stomping grounds. She has gone home where she belongs.

It's God's honest truth that we waste so much priceless time in these fleeting lives of ours centering in on the decaying, troublesome, cruel, and harmful things while in the process neglecting all the mind-boggling marvels and wonders that only God can do smack-dab in the middle of our broken pieces, shattered dreams, and fragmented pasts. We exhaust so much energy wallowing in unforgiveness, resentment, and anger, thinking we are hurting the ones that hurt us when all we are surely doing is hurling ourselves headlong into a dungeon of regret, slapping on shackles of hopelessness, chucking away the eternal for the momentary when we could be sitting in the lap of His love and grace and coming into contact with the abundant life God so desires us to have. Truly all that can ever come of un-forgiveness is a heaping helping of lost moments and an immovable mountain of regrets and sorrow.

Because of Christ, because of His forgiveness of me and His power working in and through me, I was able to forgive my mama. But I have to say that as much as anger, bitterness, and resentment are the symptoms of us declining to forgive someone I also accept as true that sometimes they just might be the source of why we cling so tightly to unforgiveness. Just sayin'.

Ephesians 4:31-32 (NIV) — *"Get rid of all bitterness, rage, and anger, brawling and slander, along with every form of malice. Be kind and compassionate to one another, forgiving each other, just as in Christ God forgave you."*

And just in case we think we might be gaining some ground in our lives by dishing out a little divine retribution upon those who have hurt us we best be soaking up our Heavenly Daddy's words of warning.

Ephesians 4:26-27 (NLT) — *"And 'don't sin by letting anger control you.' Don't let the sun go down while you are still angry, for anger gives a foothold to the devil."*

Seems to me that our all-knowing God, the Creator of heaven and earth, the all-powerful gardener of all that abounds upon it, has made it pretty apparent that by allowing these vermin to thrive in the garden of our hearts we have allowed the devil a foot in the door and the deceiver is hell-bent on contaminating the good soil of our heart when we choose anything other than to love as we have been loved by Jesus.

Romans 12:2 (NLT) — *"Don't let evil conquer you but conquer evil by doing good."*

Seems like we who say we are His just might need to shut the garden gate door to our self-seeking wants and allow our Heavenly daddy to do some weed intervention and pest control, as well as some pruning and cultivating in our overgrown gardens. God really doesn't care all that much for those stinkweeds or destructive vermin that we are so quick to allow entrance and stake a claim to our hearts. He is the Master Gardener, hallelujah! Maybe we should trust Him and not lean on our own understanding. Hmmm, when your garden smells more like it was planted downwind from an outhouse and looks like ten miles of bad road then it just might be time to lean on the expert. Trust me, I know where my gardening skills and knowledge have landed me and it ain't pretty.

Ephesians 5:1-2 ESV — *"Therefore, be imitators of God, as beloved children. And walk in love, as Christ loved us and gave himself up for us, a fragrant offering and sacrifice to God."*

I'm not perfect! Surprise! And God is never done working on this old heart of mine that is for sure. In fact, as I am writing this, God and I are having many a pow-wow about my neighbor who one night built a gun and shot two hollow point bullets through our bedroom wall. Our neighbor is scheduled to get out of prison this week and although I've said to him that I forgive him I believe there might still be some weeds of anger springing forth. I'm quite sure the anger is more about me wanting to prolong his punishment even though I've said the words, "I forgive you" to him.

Isaiah 58:11 — *"The Lord will guide you always; he will satisfy your needs in a sun-scorched land and will strengthen your frame. You will be like a well-watered garden, like a spring whose waters never fail."*

I don't think it is a coincidence that God reminded me of this verse at the very moment I was writing about my neighbor, do you? If you don't recall, this is a small part of the verses he gave me on the night when I was in my bathroom, lying in a heap on the floor and crying out to Him to help me! I just got schooled by my Holy Daddy!

Romans 6:11(MSG) — *"Could it be any clearer? Our old way of life was nailed to the cross with Christ, a decisive end to that sin-miserable life—no longer at sin's every beck and call! What we believe is this: If we get included in Christ's sin-conquering death, we also get included in his life-saving resurrection. We know that when Jesus was raised from the dead it was a signal of the end of death-as-the-end. Never again will death have the last word. When Jesus died, he took sin down with him, but alive he brings God down to us. From now on, think of it this way: Sin speaks a dead language that means nothing to you; God speaks your mother tongue, and you hang on every word. You are dead to sin and alive to God. That's what Jesus did!"*

So shut the door! You weren't born in a barn!

The first to apologize is the bravest . . .

The first to forgive is the strongest . . .

The first to forget is the happiest . . .

Never be a prisoner of your past! Turn it into a lesson and not a life sentence!

I was in the process of closing this chapter when I received a call from my husband to tell me that my neighbor was getting out of prison today. It's funny—not funny ha-ha—how my Abba Daddy works. My neighbor was going to be released two days ago but due to a mysterious illness in prisons across several states, the prison had been put on lockdown until further notice. I don't think it's a coincidence that my neighbor's freedom came about on the very day I was wrapping up this chapter of the book or that the call came almost immediately after I wrote about having to forgive him, do you? If that ain't the love of God, then I don't know what is! I guess I best be checking to make sure my door is shut! It's time to put my money where my mouth is! Ok Lord let's do this! He is the master gardener after all!

Church is out! But it is never over! Just sayin'!

CHAPTER FIVE

COME HELL OR HIGH WATER

I dream of dreams
    of fairy tales coming true
Of a knight-in-shining armor
    to carry me off into the blue
But here comes reality
    And there goes the dreams
There should be more to this life
    Then I've seen

There are no dreams in the real world
    There are no fairy tales coming true
Only the dreams of foolish young girls
    With nothing but dreaming to do

Do dreams come true
    or do they just fade away
Did my knight-in-shining armor
    get lost along the way

Tell me there is more to this life than I've seen
Then I just might start dreaming again

Katherine Bowers, age 16

I used up so much of my early years sidetracked while on a journey, searching for love, joy, and hope in all the wrong places, possessions, and people. As an insignificant starry-eyed child, I just couldn't sop up an ample amount of all the daydream-provoking, heart-fluttering, life-dodging fairy tales like Cinderella, Snow White, and such. Gosh, even Superman, a guy in a cape, would have been satisfactory for my little girl heart if there was a snowball chance of him taking his X-ray eyes off Lois Lane and setting them on me. I kid you not when I say that if anyone had posed the question, I would have crossed my heart, hoped to die, stuck a needle in my eye, and pinky sworn with fingers crossed behind my back to the cast-iron certainty that my Prince Charming was but only a heartbeat away and maybe just a tad-bit lost all because he snubbed the idea of stopping to ask for directions. Sorry, fellas!

Any hoot, I pined away for my slow-arriving and obviously detoured knight-in-shining-armor, my manly man upon a white steed, who was bound to dash wildly and whole-heartedly into my joyless existence at any second to steal me away into a grandiose sunset! Then I, like so many fortunate young damsels in distress, would have firsthand knowledge of the exhilarating enchantment of fairy-tale love and know what it means to be happy as a clam at high tide. I just knew the moment he rode into my life I'd be walking in high cotton and riding the gravy train with biscuit wheels. Woo Hoo!

In fact, all these some-day-my-prince-will-come, happily-ever-after, fairy-tales-do-come-true ramblings make me woefully wonder about what might be in store for the hardy-looking air plant that a sweet and thoughtful friend gifted me for my birthday not too many months ago. It was just the other day that I was hashing out the poor plant's distressing predicament with my double-backboned, knight-in-shining-armor hubby who snubs the notion of donning tights and has a hypersensitive reaction to horses, by letting him in on my concern that my air plant might have one foot in the grave and about to bite the dust, which is kind of funny ha-ha since it isn't even planted in soil. Any hoot, my sometimes-better-half, who is so boldfaced and brave, made up his mind to teeter on the brink of recklessly endangering his ability to suck in oxygen by chuckling at me and declaring out loud and to my face no doubt what he had evidently and so skillfully deduced over oodles of years of faithful wedlock, "That's what happens if you talk too much baby. All the oxygen gets sucked out of the air."

Good news: he is still alive! Bad news: I now know what my strategic line of defense will be if I ever need to open up some whoop on him. Hoot, there it is!

Now, if you've hung out with me an ample amount of time to really, really, really get to be on familiar terms with me then you won't be bowled over or taken aback by my husband's cheeky and ill-advised observation having to do with my competent and well-practiced knack to talk something or someone into a premature grave.

When I was at the ancient age of 18, and in a family way with my first child, I got my hands on some work at a neighboring hospital, toiling away as a clean-up specialist in their housekeeping department. While going about my day-to-day routines I became very fond of a lovable elderly gentleman whose room was on my to-do list. I honestly think he looked forward to my drop-ins and was over the moon by the socializing that would come about when I would show up to do my duties because we would gab, yak, and chitchat the entire time I was tidying up his room.

Well, it just so happened that there came a day when I was going about my daily work routine, scrubbing away in my newfound friend's bathroom, all-the-while gabbing away like there was no tomorrow and an ample amount of oxygen in the room, while he lounged in his hospital bed in the other room that I was plumb startled to death by a nurse placing her hand on my shoulder. My first thought was that she wanted me to exit the room but when I saw her finger pressed to her lips as if to say shush to me, I supposed the most obvious answer, that once again I had chatted the pleasantly kind man into a state of sweet dead-to-the-world slumber. Yes, I can do that too! My husband is my witness—or should I say victim! The nurse, with as much composure and professionalism as one could muster, given the circumstances, then quietly and tenderly as she could, updated me to the reality of my conversation-buddy's condition by softly uttering that the dear man had bit the bullet, kicked the bucket, bought the farm, and passed away while I was yakking. I was so distressed, even to the point of being speechless! Ain't that a hoot!

Well, when the females who I worked alongside of in the housekeeping unit got wind of the unpleasant incident, it was open-season on me, because they couldn't help but to cackle, tease, and harp on and on about how it was my chewing the fat and shooting the breeze that most likely led to the untimely downfall of that weak defenseless dearly-departed man. Don't giggle! It took a good bit of time for me to figure out that it was not I that had triggered his unfortunate expiration but what ailed him had finally taken its toll and brought about the timing of his inhaling his very last lung full of air. Trust me, I am pre-disposed to hot flashes of gabbing where if it was doable, I might could yak the leg off a chair, the ear off a cow, and hinges off a gate. But I have never, nay ever, chattered anyone to death! I think! I hope! Oh my! Just sayin'!

All skirting the issue and fooling aside, it's the whole truth and nothing but the truth, that banking on any one person, place, or thing to fill our joy-tank will not make us tankful! In fact, it's just the opposite for in the long run it will lead to not only sucking the verve (vitality, energy, vigor, animation, enthusiasm, life) out of our own existence but also everyone and anyone that makes; up their mind to take a stroll on the wild side and pitch a tent close by us. Shucks, I still have a stampede of hoof marks scattered across my heart and forever embedded on my great big brain because of being emotionally and verbally trampled to death by some much too close encounters with folks who deemed their joy-tank getting filled up was hinged solely upon me. Bless their heart! And if I may be frank with you, even though my name is Kathy, being around people like that is about as pleasurable as scooting on your backend britches-less through a sticker-patch brimming with poison ivy while it's raining down a horde of starved flesh-eating Texas fire ants. I kid you not!

I reckon what I'm trying to get across is that God fashioned or intended for us to have an intimate loving relationship with Him and it is out of that relationship, as we know and grow in the truth of who our Abba Daddy is, that we discover joy unspeakable, peace beyond understanding, and hope that can weather the worst of the worst this world and people are more than capable of divvying up. I'm not saying that people and circumstances won't or can't bring moments of happiness and joy to our heart and cause us to feel like we are riding the cloud-nine train! Shucks, I've had some pretty memorable moments and known some mighty marvelous people who have brought mammoth amounts of joy as well as tears-down-your-legs giddy happiness into my life. In fact, there have been times that I reckon if I felt any better, I'd drop my harp plumb through a cloud.

But most assuredly we can't, nor should we be banking on the deeds of or staking our life on the behaviors or performance of others, or even the climate of our own state of affairs in this world which can shift at the drop of a hat, to fill-up our joy-tank. What do you think would come about in your life if the filling up of your joy-tank and the condition of your emotional well-being were wholly regulated by the efforts of others and/or the coziness of your circumstances? And what pray tell will happen when the supply of these things can't even begin to live up to the demand or goodness mercy your life begins to look more like hell with everyone out to lunch? Just sayin'.

I'll never be unable to recall the first time I studied the Book of Job. Yikes I have to admit that it was somewhat unsettling to see Satan go before God and throw down the gauntlet. And it was a tad derailing when God gave the devil the go-ahead to unleash some hellish moments in poor Job's life. And it most assuredly had to be a whopping big dill to Job when he discovered himself in such a pickle! (Punny just happens!)

Job 1:8 — *"Then the LORD asked Satan, "Have you noticed my servant, Job? . . . For there is no one like him on the earth, a blameless and upright man, fearing God and turning . . . No one on earth is like him—he is a truly good person, who respects me and refuses to do evil."*

Bless his heart! Job always splits my heart of hearts into two conflicting tracks, because on the one hand, I want to be like Job and then on the other, I'd just as soon kiss a Wookie than walk in Job's shoes!

Now, I'm not gonna get into the full story of the how, what, when, and where-art-thou of Job's turbulent life but I will say Job's life makes some of those, drunk-the-day-my-mom-got-out-of-prison, blue-eyes-crying-in-the-rain, you-don't-love-me-anymore, she got-ran-over-by-a-darned ol' train country songs seem like a trip to Disney world. (No offense y'all.)

But over time, in the dark Job, the only blameless and upright man, suffered the loss of the whole shebang; every person he loved, as well as his comfort and health. Well, he almost lost everyone! Everyone that is but his ill-informed and not-so-helpful wife who haphazardly put forward some not-so-wise counsel as a solution or way out of her hubby's agony by telling suffering Job, "Curse God and die". Yep, I want that good ol' girl hanging out in my neck of the woods, standing in my corner, and filling my joy-tank the next time life smacks me upside of the head with a two-by-four. Don't you! And if all Job's possessions, loved ones, and health were what he was counting on to load up his joy-tank to the brim then he would have been up the creek without a paddle for he couldn't even put it in his pipe and smoke it because he would have only discovered that he was just sucking on fumes.

Oh, and I'd have to slap myself into next Tuesday if I overlooked or turned my back on Job's due-diligent buddies, who show up in the middle of Job's world-going-to-hell-in-a-handbasket crisis while he is grief-stricken over the loss of all his family, property, wealth, status and health. I'm just gonna say it because I know you are thinking it too! Those frenemies were about as useful as a skunk at a lawn party. If you've never read the book of Job and have a huge hankering to do so, then I would suggest and encourage you to step away from my rattling-on long enough to do so. Go ahead! I'll wait!

Now let's sit for a spell and have a pow-wow about Job's insensitive and rash so-called friends. Honest-to-Pete, I still wrestle with the eye-popping, anger-inducing, jaw-dropping realization that Job's friends just parked themselves on a bench, for seven days and seven nights, eyeballing Job up one end and down the other, all the while not speaking one word of comfort or hope. In hindsight, I now see it as a blessing. And what a circus and a performance it is when they at last unlocked their jaws and all they could manage to barf up or spit out was, "Job, you've sinned! You're going to have to confess and get right, or God is never going to return you to His favor". If Job had been a Texan, I'm pretty sure those good ol' boys would have been wearing their teeth as a necklace. But He was an upright man and not prone to evil! Job's friends should thank God for that! Praiseallujah!

Being from Texas I can't help but get a bitter taste in my mouth when I think about their behavior because those good ol' boys remind me of vultures perching on a limb, waiting for a fellow to expire just so they can pick his bones clean. Now Job's frenemies, who apparently were all-knowing as well as compassionate, deduced that everything going on with and to Job was because he must have done wrong against God and was out of God's good grace. What I do love about the saga of Job, not sure if I should say that out loud, is that although Job had lost his entire family of nearest and dearest except for his helpmate who wasn't much help, all his livestock, worldly goods, and possessions, and is seated in ashes and scraping at the oozing, foul-smelling, excruciating boils with shards of pottery, he still turns down the not-so-wise-suggestion by his woman to curse God. Hmmm, it seems like the filling up of his joy-tank, as well as the level of his faith barometer, was not hitched to the wagon of his circumstances or the people in his life at all. Ain't that a hoot!

Now, don't get me wrong! If you read the book of Job you will see where there did come a time when Job had questions for God and even wished he had gone on to meet his maker but if Job's joy-tank was determined by getting his itch scratched (whoops) or by God answering all his questions, then even there he would have found himself running on empty, for God did not address the why-me or what-for of the state of affairs Job found himself submerged in. God's comeback to Job was to make clear to Job the facts of God's workings and His character instead of educating Job on the subject matter of why he was in such a pickle or the when, what, or why of all his affliction and misfortune. God's answer to Job's situation was Himself, His character, His faithfulness, and His power! What really wobbled my world to the knees of my heart was when Job said, while in the depths of his gloom, despair, and agony, and in the absence of fleshy backup, "Though He slay me I will trust Him!"

I have to ponder on this for a spell and quietly tiptoe around the speculation that if Job's life had never had an intermission from the so-called good life and a separation from the things that could inadvertently be fueling his joy-tank, then maybe he would have never come to the point where he would be able to say without hesitation or doubt, "Though He slay me I will trust Him."

Psalm 37:3-5 Amplified Bible (AMP) —
"Trust [rely on and have confidence] in the LORD and do good;
Dwell in the land and feed [securely] on His faithfulness.
Delight yourself in the LORD,
And He will give you the desires and petitions of your heart.
Commit your way to the LORD;
Trust in Him also and He will do it.
Trust in the Lord!"

I love, love, love the Hebrew language because it portrays and renders some of the most splendiferous works of art you could ever conjure up. The chief meaning of the word trust that is used here goes back to the notion of literally someone who is defenselessly stretched out, face down on the floor. Prostrate! There's that word again! It is the frame of mind and position of a person who has come to the limit of their entire where-withal, state of affairs, family or friends and has no support system. It is total reliance and dependence upon God! I think it's safe to say that Job was smack-dab in the middle of that one! Job's faith in God is so strong he makes Samson look sensitive.

Now if you are like me, you are either fighting the notion or gently tiptoeing through the tulips and around the question of how any of us can get to the place of trusting God even if . . . ! I don't mean to be a smarty-pants or claim to know it all, but I think there may be only one way to get there! And that is by trusting God! It's just that simple and that challenging!

Now I'm not saying any of the great books, scholars, etc. . . . that we have access to are harmful, but I just don't think in this instance that we can learn to trust God by leafing through books and reading on how to trust Him. You don't learn to trust God by pinning your ears back and listening to sermons on trusting Him either. You can only be taught to trust God by acting upon what He says! Now, I don't know about you, but I didn't learn to drive a car by reading books on cars, did you? Yes, I did learn the rules of the road by reading but the only way for me to really learn to drive required that I literally get in the car, start it up, and pull out of the driveway, onto the road and drive. I reckon if the only way to learn to trust God is by taking a step of faith and trusting Him then truth-be told most of us won't trust God until we have to trust Him. Ouch! And for some of us it just might not be till we have no other choice and find ourselves in a place where we must determine and choose to trust God. Honestly, wouldn't you rather move when God calls you than have Him move you! Now you might want to plug your ears for this next part because it might bite and sting a tad bit!

God is an expert at seeing to it that we must trust Him and He will educate us on how to trust Him. Yikes, that sounds about as easy as putting socks on a rooster.

But God . . .

Not so long ago I came across the phrase, "shut up to faith." When I heard that saying it really got me to mulling over a whole lot of thoughts.

Shut up to faith! When all is said and all is done it means God will permit us, this is gonna hurt a wee bit y'all, even move us, say it ain't so, into conditions where there is no other route out but up, blessing or curse, live or die, trust God or go down. Shut up to Faith! Sounds about as comfortable as hugging a rose bush.

But God . . .

An eye-catching likeness of the statement, "shut up to faith," is when the Israelites noticed themselves parked on the banks of the Red Sea after Moses, who was under God's direction, had broken them out of their shackles and imprisonment as slaves, rescued them out of Egypt and brought them pitch a tent by the Red Sea!

Exodus 14:1-2 — *"Now the LORD spoke to Moses, saying, "Tell the sons of Israel to turn back and camp before Pi-hahiroth, (Pie, ha-hiroth) between Migdol and the sea; you shall camp in front of Baal-zephon, opposite it, by the sea. For Pharaoh will say of the sons of Israel, 'They are wandering aimlessly in the land; the wilderness has shut them in.' Thus, I will harden Pharaoh's heart, and he will chase after them; and I will be honored through Pharaoh and all his army, and the Egyptians will know that I am the LORD."*

Truth-be-told the Israelites were following God who had led them to this point! He maneuvered them into this situation. Now they were shut in by the wilderness or the boondocks as I like to call it. They were shut up to faith and the only way out was to go back in the same direction of the herd of angry Egyptians on their tail or to look up, trust God, and rely upon His faithfulness.

Paint this picture in your mind!

You have just been liberated, emancipated, delivered from and out of 430 years of bondage. Woo Hoo! You are following the divine, all-knowing guidance and leading of God and now find yourself on a nature hike and pitching a tent in the very place God told you to. All is right with the world. The Red Sea in all its wonder and force is in front of you, the mountains in their grandiose splendor on either side of you and Egypt, your pint-sized piece of hell on earth is in your rearview mirror. That is, until the day you wake up, peek over your shoulder, and see moving toward you, hell-bent on putting some major hurt on you, a whole lot of chain-loving, whip-snapping, hangry Egyptians swooping down on you like a herd of riled-up buffalo.

What ya gonna do when they come for you?

Run!

There is nowhere to run!

Hide!

There is nowhere to hide!

Play dead!

Doesn't even work for possums, y'all!

Exodus 14:11-12 — *"Then they said to Moses, "Is it because there were no graves in Egypt that you have taken us away to die in the wilderness? Why have you dealt with us in this way, bringing us out of Egypt? Is this not the word that we spoke to you in Egypt, saying, leave us alone that we may serve the Egyptians'? For it would have been better for us to serve the Egyptians than to die here in the wilderness?"*

Ain't that a hoot! Those Israelites can't get no satisfaction, oh but they tried! They are as disoriented as a redhead in a round room looking for a corner (sorry redheads, I should have approached that more gingerly) so they start complaining and blaming Moses. Forgive my Texanese or Tex-message paraphrasing y'all!

"Moses, you underhanded dog, I reckon this is one heck of a pickle you done got us all into. If we hadn't paid you no never mind we could've been laying on the front porch with the rebellious, God-denying Egyptian dogs, scratching our fleas, and living high on the hog under the dung of their oppressive yoke of bowing down to man-made, impotent little g's, all comfy-cozy in our well-worn chains and satisfied by our routines and what we are used to. But no, you had to haul us out into the unknown and now we are going to croak!"

Exodus 14:13-14 (AMP) — *"Then Moses said to the people, 'Do not be afraid! Take your stand [be firm and confident and undismayed] and see the salvation of the LORD which He will accomplish for you today; for those Egyptians whom you have seen today, you will never see again. The LORD will fight for you while you [only need to] keep silent and remain calm.'"*

Since we are being genuine here, I have to point out that if I were Moses, someone would be getting the rod and the staff! Just sayin'. But Moses is so kind, so long-suffering, and unflappable that he speaks to the people and reminds them of the God that has steered them out of their captivity and has been alongside them from the get-go.

I so love Exodus 14:13-14, but I must plead guilty that I have moments (yes, I admit that I don't always have it altogether) when life gives the impression that it is going to hell in a handbasket, and honest-to-Pete my first reaction is not to stay calm and most certainly not to be silent. I'm not a hand wringer like my grandmother, who would walk up and down, back and forth while wringing her hands and saying, 'Lordy, Lordy.' No, I'm more of a "you want a piece of me" kind of girl! You might ask what's wrong with that! Well, nothing, as long as I realize I can't fight this battle on my own, nor should I, and that I have this big and mighty, ever-faithful, more than capable God Who fights on my behalf.

One of my favorite sayings is, "never wrestle with a pig, you both get dirty, and the pig likes it." Well, when I try to fight a battle on my own I end up plastered in the stinky muck of this world by jumping over God's perfect fence line, trampling all over His trustworthy heart, and smelling like crap, all because I chose to descend into the pigpen and roll in the dung and muck only to end up looking and smelling no different than the pig I wrestled.

Disclaimer again: I have nothing against pigs.

Now my other go-to reaction when in trouble or afraid is to scream and run. Trust me, when I run from what scares me instead of running to the One who can slay the Goliaths or the Egyptians in my life, I tend to plow down a few unintended bystanders along the way. It's a constant struggle to shut my mouth and remain calm while the God of Angel armies fights on my behalf. Maybe you can relate.

Any hoot let's get back to the hemmed-in Israelites. In their shut-up-to-faith moment our sweet and all-knowing God says hush your mouth children, stop your whining, get your eyes off your problem and back on me where they belong. What are a few hundred man-made chariots and some riled-up wood-worshipping Egyptian warriors got that I ain't got and that I ain't able to God-handle. I AM God! I've got this! Let me fight the fight, you need only be silent. (Gulp) Can I just say how convicted and convinced I am right now about my jaw-jacking ways! Whoa! Honest to Pete, when I run from what scares me instead of running to the One who can slay the Goliaths in my life, I tend to plow down a few innocent bystanders along the way. There it is! Oh Lord help me to remember that I need only be silent and remain calm for the God of Angel armies fights on my behalf.

Now our first inclination, based on fear of out-of-our-control situations and lack of understanding of the God that is in control of what is out of our control, is to shout out, "God, what were you thinking and why did you let it get this far? If only You . . ."

You know I can't always get what I want. Truthfully what I want may not be what I need. What I want and think I need just might be hinged on my comfort and not my growth. God cares more about our righteousness than He does our comfort!

Exodus 14:4: — *"I will harden Pharaoh's heart so that he will pursue them. Then I will receive glory by means of Pharaoh and all his army, and the Egyptians will know that I am Yahweh."*

Our difficulty is that when we don't always know the why, what-for, and/or when of our tight spot we just give up the ghost, turn tail, and make a mad dash, whine, complain, and blame, when what we need to do is trust that no matter what, God is up to something beneficial and first-rate, we need only be silent. We need to trust in the nature and promises of God and that He is the answer even when we don't have all the answers. Ouch again! Be still and know that He is God! I think we all forget that one sometimes! Be still and know (act upon the truth) that I AM God!

Exodus 6:6 — *"Say, therefore, to the sons of Israel, 'I am the LORD, and I will bring you out from under the burdens of the Egyptians, and I will deliver you from their bondage. I will also redeem you with an outstretched arm and with great judgments.'"*

God allows this one moment in time (the song just flitted across my mind) so that He will be given the glory so fittingly due Him. The idol-weighed-down, blinded-by-the-darkness Egyptians will recognize that He is THE Lord (Jehovah, Yahweh, the One and only, no one greater, no one higher) and in that He will make it very clear to Israel that He is their rock, deliverer, and salvation. You know getting the Israelites out of Egypt seems a tad bit easier than getting 430 years of Egypt out of them, doesn't it!

God works in some out-of-this-world, out-of-the-box ways.

He could have smitten the wheels off the Egyptian's chariots, ditching them, and leaving them high and dry in the desert to waste away . . .

But God . . .

He could have hurled a cloud of rattlesnakes to alarm the horses of the Egyptians . . .

But God . . .

He could have launched an angel taskforce to take out the entire band of rebels . . .

But God . . .

But God funneled Israel into a close-fitting space, literally between a rock and a hard place, a situation that was without an explanation or any observable way out to break out from by human ways or means, so that they would lie face down before Him, reliant upon Him as they experience the fact that He is the God that saves, and give up walking in this world like they were still bound, shackled slaves in Egypt. And He also stirred about in such a way that those wayward, rebellious, and little blind idol-worshipping Egyptians would be friendly with the fact that they were barking up the wrong tree and messing with the One and Only, true God! And He did it for His holy name! Wow!

Deuteronomy 8:2 — *"You shall remember all the way which the LORD your God has led you in the wilderness these forty years, that He might humble you, testing you, to know what was in your heart, whether you would keep His commandments or not."*

God is saying to Israel, "I was after something in you! You were made for more! "I brought you into these conditions so you could practice what you preach, put your money where your mouth is, put up or shut up! God doesn't want us to be a bunch of gum-bumpers. But it is also in those tightly-squeezed places, those shut-up-to-faith instants that we can discover and know who the "God of angel armies" truly is and what He and He alone is more than able and capable of undertaking. God is telling the Israelites that only their unadulterated, out-and-out trust in Him can ever get them out! So, the Egyptians inch closer in the direction of the Israelites, and there is nowhere to run and nowhere to hide for one or the other side.

Exodus 14:10 — *"As Pharaoh drew near, the sons of Israel looked, and behold, the Egyptians were marching after them, and they became very frightened; so, the sons of Israel cried out to the LORD."*

Imagine this! You've got your whole clan with you: your children, grandchildren, uncles, aunts, nieces, nephews . . . the whole kit and caboodle, all that matters to you, when your ears pick up the sounds of the terrifying, fear-provoking, and all too familiar grumble of the Egyptian's chariot wheels, the jingling of their swords and their vicious war cries.

Y'all God understands our fear! I mean why else would he say over and over in His word, "Do not be afraid". Truth-be-told, I think God would have been tickled pink through and through if instead of succumbing to their fear the Israelites would have sent a prayer upward instead of focusing on the rearview mirror. Imagine if they had cried out to God, secure in His faithfulness and trusting in His power, "Lord we're terrified out of our britches! We are shaking in our sandals, but we are so very aware of the fact that You and only You are the one who removed our shackles of slavery and delivered us up and out of the Egyptian's hands, and You will be trustworthy once again. When we were in Egypt You rescued us from the angel of death and from all the plagues that showed the Egyptians that their little-g-idols made of wood are nothing but man-made pick-up-sticks and only fitting and useful for kindle in the fire. And we know that You have the clout and the muscle to hand us over or to deliver us from our enemies now. So, Father, the God Who sees, Who knows, and Who is able, more than able to redeem us once again from our enemies, we are positioning our lives, our children's lives, our grandchildren, everything in your hands right now . . ."

Nope! That's not what they did!

Instead, they pointed fingers at Moses and not only that, but they also charged God, the one who set them free, with trying to wipe them out of existence. Yikes!

So, there the frightened Israelites find themselves- "shut up to faith". They have a choice, just as we do—to trust God or die. And God says trust Me and see the salvation of the Lord! Move forward and take possession of the land! But one problem, y'all—they have this big honking sea looming before them. Sometimes we just can't see our Abba Daddy for the sea! Oh oh! We shout out for the map and want a complete picture of the trek ahead before we will round the next bend. We want to see the full picture on the puzzle box of our life. We just have to know where every piece goes and what it will look like but I'm not so sure we could handle knowing the rest of the story and what lies before us!

We say we believe! Even the demons believe and tremble! Gosh some of us say we believe, and we don't do anything, even tremble. Now I don't know about you but who would have ever thunk that God would split the Red Sea, which is no puddle, down the middle. Truth-be-told, if I were those Israelites, I probably would have been eyeing the horizon looking for the nearest ferry before I would be thinking God is going to split a sea that is over 190 miles across at its widest point, and about

1,200 miles in length. Do you think anyone turned to God and yelled, "Oh God, you do realize there is a sea in front of us?" Now you don't want to miss this next part.

Psalms 114:3 — *"And the waters fled before them."*

The waters fled before them! I don't know about you, but I could sit still for that! If that isn't enough to give evidence to the power and faithfulness of God, then I don't know what is! The big, powerful Red Sea fled, and the Israelites strolled across like a walk in the park on dry land. Not damp nor wet, but dry land! It's funny—not funny ha-ha—that for some of us that is precisely what it has taken or what it will take for us to trust God. An Egyptian army on our tail and a Red Sea planted before us. So shut up to faith that we must trust God and live or . . . !

Within months after I had put my heart in the hands of the One who stills the water, I found myself gawking at my Red Sea and shut up to faith. As if having to tell my daughter I love her wasn't enough to say Lord, I trust You then the sea God allowed to be positioned before me was probably one of the most frightening and challenging trials that I could imagine—at least at that time. I say that now because I had no inkling as to what was to follow only a couple of years later down the road. Before I even had what I thought would be ample enough time to come to grips with the things of my past as well as allowing God to adjust my heart toward my mom she came up from Texas to pay a visit for a spell. Things were going pretty well, all things considered, until about midway into her stay when my Mama came to me and told me that my knight-in-shining-armor, my joy-tank filler hubby, had voiced to her that he was going to issue an ultimatum to me.

The day I came home from surrendering my life to Christ I had shared with my husband what God had done the night before on that bathroom floor and the next day when I walked into His church. And although I was fully aware of my husband's commitment and that He loved me to the moon and back and to infinity and beyond I also knew that he wanted no part of what he called "organized religion". I won't go there right now. But I do have to say it would crack me up when he would say he was a non-practicing catholic. Of course, me being the stand-up, sit-down comedian that I am, I always had to jump in and plug a few funnies about how much practice would be enough for him to get into heaven if he did begin practicing once again! Yikes! Needless to say, he didn't see the funny or punny side of my jokes.

Any hoot, before Christ, my world orbited around the people and things in it. My joy-tank was filled by accomplishments, acquiring things, and the people who loved me as well as drained by the exact opposite. After Christ moved into my heart, God began to move in mighty ways, and it was like every day He was spring-cleaning my heart. Boy, did He have His hands full. In the evening, I would spend hours in my office praying, singing and writing. Then I would move to the front porch and spend another couple of hours there just talking and listening for God's voice. I didn't even grasp how much God meant to me but apparently it was becoming uncomfortably noticeable more and more to my knight-in-shining-armor. I never really read too much into the look on my husband's face that Sunday when I came home and told him I had yielded my life to Christ. But now that I think about it, I'm pretty sure it was not so much a look of skepticism but fear that I saw briefly flash across his face.

Any hoot, my mama came to me a few days before she was to fly back home to Texas and told me that she was concerned for our marriage and that my knight-in-shining-armor had told her he was going to ask me to choose between him and God. I can still hear the growling wheels of the enemy's chariot behind me and the sea waters raging before me as a storm of fear began to swell up in my heart. I was hemmed in on both sides! After she had delivered the news, I did the only thing I knew to do. I went into my office, locked the door, and cried. My husband was the one and only person in my life that I knew loved me unconditionally. I remember right before meeting him praying that God would send someone into my life who could love me as much as I am capable of loving them. Then into my life he rode, my knight-in-shining-armor, minus the horse and the tights, sweeping me off my weary feet, rescuing me from my dungeon of despair, and whisking me away to a far-away land in the north (New Jersey) where I really didn't speak the language, and away from all that tortured and caused me pain. I guess if anyone had asked me what filled my joy-tank, I probably would have answered with my husband.

There I was shut up in my office, face to face with God and my worst fear and having to choose between the love of this life and the love of eternity. The enormity of what my mom had shared with me sucked all the oxygen out of my lungs, my heart began to ache and groan, my eyes began to leak tears and the dam of pent-up emotions burst forth as I collapsed from the pure weightiness of it all, dropping down on my knees. Right there and then I began to cry and plead with God, "Please don't make me choose, please don't make me choose!"

I was shut up to faith! The Egyptians were biting at my heels and the Red Sea was at high tide and looming before me and the only way out was up, blessing or curse, live or die, trust God or drown. And then, before I even knew the thought had formed in my head, my heart poured out words that were so foreign to what my head could even comprehend, "Father God, I love You and I love him. Please don't make me choose! But God, if I gotta choose, I choose You!"

As the words that I could have never ever imagined saying spilled out of my mouth, I sprawled out on the floor sobbing like crazy while I prayed and praised my heavenly Abba daddy. It honestly blew my mind to realize how much I loved my Heavenly Father, and it rocked my world to know that I relied upon and trusted in His love for me that much. I can't even begin to explain it!

It's true that God knew what was in my heart that day, but I could have never fathomed how much He meant to me had it not been for the opportunity to be shut up to faith! My joy-tank was filled to the brim with the God who saved me, and my faith barometer increased in a grand Texas-size measure. I did not mention the chat between my mom and myself to my hubby but instead chose to wait out my time for the moment when he would choose to deal out his ultimatum.

One Sunday, a few months down the road a spell, I was getting dressed for church when my pookie-bear jumped up out of bed and began to put on his nice duds. I asked him why he was getting dressed up and to my shock and surprise he said he was planning on going to church with me. Now, I'm not saying this was the clued-up comeback, but it was mine, for I quickly answered back not with giddy excitement but with angst-ridden wariness, "Uh, you don't go to church!"

It's a God thing y'all, because after my lukewarm response he still went to church with me! Praiseallujah!

After that Sunday, my knight showed up for church off and on, made a number of fascinating observations as well as some not-so-prince-charming-like remarks, all the while making sure He kept his distance by attempting to build a roadblock to halt those who threatened to overrun his breathing space and display to him the love of Jesus. I guess you could say he was shut up to faith too! But God... has a way of moving, maneuvering, and operating in ways that can boggle our mind, make our teeter totter, and knock our socks off so that every opportunity to share Christ in word and deed is not squandered or pointless, that is for sure.

It was the week before Christmas of that very same year of the ultimatum dilemma, that I was kneeling at the altar at church and praying with a dear woman, when I began to hear an exorbitant amount of crying, more than usual, and a bit of a to-do going on behind me. I tried to take no notice of whatever was going on in the background and center in on the woman I was praying with, but the unexplained and unidentified commotion was making it awfully challenging. That is, until I felt a strong hand rest on my shoulder and turned around to see my pastor attending to our weeping son. That's when the pastor, who was also tearful, shared with me that my baby boy of eighteen years had just handed over his life over to Jesus. I knelt there at the altar, a mom whose heart was spilling over with unspeakable joy and began to shed tears and pray over my once-lost but now-found one-and-only son. That is until I was sidetracked once again by an even rowdier chorus of sobbing and bawling like I had heard before. I couldn't even begin to conjure up in my mind's eye what kind of incident might cause such an all-fired ruckus as was going on behind me, but I was bent on praying with my baby. That's when I felt a hand on my shoulder yet again. I truly had no inkling what I might find so when I turned around and saw my sweet husband standing beside my smiling and teary-eyed pastor and bawling like a fella who didn't care if other fellas saw him crying, I almost gave up the ghost, bit the dust, and bought the farm. I was not prepared for and baffled by my husband's intense and unexplained emotions as well as the pastor's flabbergasting words when he told me that my knight-in-shining-armor minus the tights, had just deposited his trust and his very life into the ever-loving nail-pierced hands of Jesus, our Savior. And just like that, the waters fled, and my Red Sea parted! I was bowled over and rendered speechless! Cross my heart and hope to spit!

When we are shut up to faith, moving forward even when the sea looms before us, and there appears to be no way around it, then it is evidence to others that we are depending upon our God who is beyond trustworthy. And it makes observable to the Egyptians, the Goliaths, and the demons that are nipping at our heels that our confidence is in the one true God, the God of angel armies Who fights on our behalf. We need only be silent.

And maybe, just maybe when we are shut up to faith, we need our memory jogged by bringing to mind that the One who wages war on our behalf is beyond a shadow of doubt more than competent and qualified to handle our battles. I don't know who penned the following reading but it is so picture-painting-perfect and something worth bringing to mind the next time you're "shut up to faith" and sense your hope in His promises waning, your reliance upon His muscle, supremacy, and workings wobbling, your joy-tank running on a quarter of a tank heading toward empty, and your confidence in His all-powerful and faithful reputation in short supply of commitment.

Before the earth and water burst forth . . . . This is our God!
With a Word, He spoke. Creation arose . . . . . . This is our God!
The Red Sea parted, kept His people free . . . . . This is our God!
The walls of Jericho came crashing down . . . . . This is our God!
A barren woman's prayer was heard . . . . This is our God!
A boy, a stone, a giant killed. . . . . This is our God!
Fierce lions could not harm a praying man. . . . This is our God!
Fire unable to burn three mortals . . . . This is our God!
The God of Abraham, Isaac, and Jacob. . . . . . . This is our God!
Born in a stable, as a peasant He came . . . . This is our God!
Water turned into choice wine . . . . This is our God!

Five loaves, two fish, thousands fed . . . . This is our God!

The One who prays and intercedes for us . . . . . This is our God!

The God-man who bled and died for us . . . . . . This is our God!

Defeating death, He rose and lives . . . . This is our God!

The King of Kings gives life to us . . . . This is our God!

In His presence, the darkness flees . . . . This is our God!

The One we will be with for eternity . . . . This is our God!

So that mind-blowing Sunday the heavens quaked with laughter, delight, and celebration as the angels applauded and whooped it up in heaven and hell trembled with foreboding terror and anguish as the demonic forces screeched and pitched a hissy fit times four because of the rescue and deliverance of my hubby and son from its evil clutches. Woo Hoo! Put that in your pipe and smoke it Satan!

When we returned back home that afternoon, it was then that I let my pookie-bear in on the fact that my mom had let the cat out of the bag and dropped a Texas-size hailstone on my world by tipping me off about his distress-triggering ultimatum. It took the wind out of my lungs when I saw that my hubby was not only taken aback and downright flabbergasted by my mom's disclosure of such a stipulation but also doggedly adamant that he had by no means, under no circumstances and at no time, not ever, nay never voiced those words to her. Ain't that a hoot!

It makes no never mind the how, what, or why of the incident because I am so beholden to my God allowing that chapter in my life where I found myself shut up to faith and squeezed between a rock and a hard place all because I believed that I was going to have to choose between my knight-in—shining-armor that I had always dreamed of and my love-giving, hope-stimulating, grace-granting, soul-redeeming, joy-tank supplying, heart-healing sacrificial One-and-only King.

Without being subjected to that ground zero flare-up in my life, where I was shut up to faith, I don't think I would know the measure of my passion for and/or my faith in Him nor be able to proclaim with such assurance and faith; "though He slay me I will trust Him", come hell or high water! Little did I know that hell and high water were coming around the bend.

But God . . .

Exodus 14:13-14 (AMP) — *"Do not be afraid! Take your stand [be firm and confident and undismayed] and see the salvation of the Lord which He will accomplish for you today; for those Egyptians whom you have seen today, you will never see again. The Lord will fight for you while you [only need to] keep silent and remain calm."*

CHAPTER SIX

THE PORCH LIGHT IS ALWAYS BURNING

My adventurous faith-enlarging journey has indeed steered me down many a path where I have come face to face with the mind-blowing and caring works of my Abba Daddy while in the weightiness of some of the most challenging, white-knuckled, hair-raising, nerve-wracking, spine-tingling, breathtaking, heartening, giddy, awakening, and exhilarating stretches of my days. But if you had informed me that I just might come to learn more about my Abba Daddy's character and actions from zip-lining, I would have more than likely supposed that you just might be about as crazy as a bullbat.

In case you don't know, I wasn't birthed double-backboned and that is a fact. Trust me! So, to my surprise, I found myself positioned upright on a wooden perch, suspended high up in the middle of swaying trees while linked to a cable that appeared to only run from one measly platform to another and that I was pretty sure my grandma would have said was only good for stringing up laundry! If that wasn't scary enough, the few cords and clamps secured around my quivering body to keep me from snapping my neck and shattering every bone in my frame didn't resonate with me so well nor was jumping from a perfectly good landing seeming like the most levelheaded or sane thing to do, let alone the safest. Oh, but isn't it so like our Heavenly Father to school us smack dab in the middle of our what-was-I thinking, this-is-not-what-I-fixed-my-face-for, I'd-just-as-soon-bite-a-bug, I-don't-cotton-to-it, put-your-big-girl-panties-on-and-deal-with-it moments.

I can't quite recollect how my first zip-lining undertaking came about but I'm somewhat sure it originated from and came to fruition because of an exchange my hubby and I were having one day with our spontaneous and adventuresome friends, Stan and Lynda. Needless to say, one thing led to another and voila, there I was, plunked at death's door, situated on a man-made perch in the woods. I was so high up it made me wish I had been born with wings, buckled in like a newborn baby in a car seat with my knees quaking, heart hammering like I had a chest full of woodpeckers, my voice a pitch or two higher than usual, yakking so quickly that I could have taken to the air on my own wind, face bleached as white as grandma's sheets, and trying to take a really good stab at talking myself down off a perfectly sound ledge. Cross my heart and hope to spit, if that ain't a special kind of crazy I just don't know what is!

While I was poised there on my high-in-the sky perch, teetering on the brink of hurdling straight into the presence of my Jesus, the youthful and very patient flight instructor was giving it a good go at coaching me on the proper and fitting way to leap to my demise. All the while my not-so-persuasive buddies and hubby were trying to tenderly wheedle and sweet-talk me into making like Tarzan by stepping onto thin air. Honest-to-Pete, the accommodating co-conspirators to my murder might have had a better shot at coaxing me to charge hell with a bucket of ice water than getting me to step off into thin air with not even the tiniest glimpse of dry land in sight.

Now mind you I know this might be questionable, but I wasn't born yesterday and nor was I born on a funny farm for that matter! And I reckon I do have enough uncommon common sense to spit downwind, find my way out of a paper bag, and to know which end is up. And because I hail from the grand ol' country of Texas, where sushi is still called bait, I certainly do know diddly squat and had utterly grasped one very vital piece of information; if I plunged to the ground, I was not gonna miss! And it's a well-known fact that you can't fix that kind of stupid with duct tape!

Honest-to-Pete, if my grandma had been gazing on—God rest her soul—she would have been at her wit's end, madder than a rattler in a rainstorm, wringing her hands, and pitching a hissy fit while hollering, "Katherine Mae did you hit your head? You were too hard to raise to take chances!"

Hoot there it is! And with that notion frolicking in my great brain, I launched into an intensive and painstaking assessment of my precarious and dicey condition. Faster than a duck on a June bug, I could feel acute rigor mortis settling into my bones resulting in me being gravely frozen in my spot and scared so stiff that I was touching cotton (translation put delicately; about to have tears run down my legs). Trust me when I say that in my what-was-I-thinking moment, there was a better likelihood of Congress passing an act in one day than me taking a flying leap off the tower of terror. I kid you not! If I had my druthers, I'd be sitting down below, snacking on popcorn, thoroughly entertained and tranquil as I watched other victims of stupidity grapple with their put-up or shut-up, life-or-death moment.

I must fess up and say that I have been utterly and out-and-out blessed with some of the most terribly obliging and longsuffering friends in all of God's creation! My considerate friend Lynda, who has a lot of snap in her garters (she's capable y'all), was more than willing and able to accommodate my dying wish by forcing herself to undertake the grueling mission of helping things along by giving me the tender and proper nudge I so greatly required and most likely deserved. Ain't that a hoot! Bless her heart!

You can take it to the bank and cash it when I say publicly that not only did zip-lining give me a faith-lift, but it also upgraded my prayer life to a cloud-nine status. Cause don't you know when this girl broke wind (you know what I mean) all my mind could call up in that split second was, "Yea though I fly through the valley of the shadow of death I will fear no evil for You are with me. Please don't let me die, Lord! Please don't let me die!"

Truth-be-told, the thorniest piece about my zip-lining escapade was letting go! When I say letting go, I mean stepping off the fixed and reliable platform of what I could see and trusting in what I could not! And who would have thought that looking down instead of gazing up just made matters that much more unpleasant! Wow, I must say perspective really is the whole ball of wax because the instant I was ever so kindly shoved off the platform of my fear and airborne I was subjected to sweet freedom as I plummeted through the tall trees as fast as a hot knife through butter.

Now I reckon I will come clean and say that my initial reaction to my death-defying feat was not to cheer but to squeal like a pig being rounded up for slaughter. But once I recognized that I was snug as a bug in a rug, flying through the brisk air and not kissing the ground with my face, I was in hog heaven and hallelujahing the countryside. I had an epiphany that day! I realized that just because I couldn't see the ground for the trees it didn't mean that the ground wasn't there. Just because I didn't understand how I was being carried along during the risky venture didn't mean that I was on my own!

It's funny—not funny ha-ha—that as I have been penning this chapter, God has been inundating me with message upon message that reiterates all that I have survived and what I've experienced to be so absolutely true about His goodness. The following scripture came up in my devotional as well as in a sermon series that started at our church about a week after I began to write about perspective, the unseen, and my Abba Daddy. Ain't that so God! So, we best get to unpacking His truth.

2 Kings 6:8-17 (MSG) — *"One time when the king of Aram was at war with Israel, after consulting with his officers, he said, 'At such and such a place I want an ambush set.'*

"The Holy Man (Elisha) sent a message to the king of Israel: 'Watch out when you're passing this place, because Aram has set an ambush there.'

"So, the king of Israel sent word concerning the place of which the Holy Man had warned him.

"This kind of thing happened all the time.

"The king of Aram was furious over all this. He called his officers together and said, 'Tell me, who is leaking information to the king of Israel? Who is the spy in our ranks?'

"But one of his men said, 'No, my master, dear king. It's not any of us. It's Elisha the prophet in Israel. He tells the king of Israel everything you say, even what you whisper in your bedroom.'

"The king said, 'Go and find out where he is. I'll send someone and capture him.'

"The report came back, 'He's in Dothan.'"

Well needless to say, it's easy to see that it is about to get as ugly as Grandpa's toenails, cause the King of Aram has his tail up and is in a horn-tossing mood. . . .

"Then he (King of Aram) dispatched horses and chariots, an impressive fighting force. They came by night and surrounded the city.

"Early in the morning a servant of the Holy Man got up and went out. Surprise! Horses and chariots surrounding the city! The young man exclaimed, 'Oh, master! What shall we do?'"

Well, that dog won't hunt for Elisha! Elisha is as brave as the first man to eat an oyster and ready to take his stand against the enemy hordes.

Excuse my squirrel chasing, but I love Isaiah 61:3, and I can't help but think about what God says He is going to give his people; *"the oil of gladness instead of mourning. The garment of praise instead a spirit of fainting so they will be called oaks of righteousness, the planting of the Lord, that He may be glorified."* Hoot there it is!

I can't help but recall and giggle a bit at a cute little quote I once got wind of, "A great oak is only a little nut that stood its ground." Someday I too hope to be a little less of a nut and a whole lot more of an oak! Woo Hoo!

Oh, but to the shaking-in-his-drawers servant, Elisha just might have given the notion that he is several nuts shy of a bushel and had lost his pea-picking mind. But "great oak" Elisha knows that the ground he is standing on is holy and that there are truly angels all around. It is so plain to see that nothing and no one is situated in the way of Elisha's sightline of God's presence, power, or promises, for in one-half less than no time, Elisha is heaven-bent on jogging the memory of the forgetful, far-sighted and fussing servant about the heavenly truth of their present state of affairs.

Elisha said, "Don't worry about it—there are more on our side than on their side."

Elisha, all unruffled, cool, and composed as a cucumber, encourages the servant by saying, "Don't worry about it" and announces that "those who are with us are more than those who are with them."

Then Elisha prayed, "O GOD, open his eyes and let him see."

I pray these very words all the time for those who are blinded by the little g of this world! O God, open their eyes so that they may see! I pray this for myself and my family of God too when we so oftentimes catch ourselves shut up to faith and blinded by what we feel instead of trusting in what we cannot often see!

The eyes of the young man were opened, and he saw. A wonder! The whole mountainside full of horses and chariots of fire surrounding Elisha!

A WONDER! Now I could sit still for that!

How like the God of angel armies to take a disturbance of the foulest kind and turn it into a WONDER of the divine kind. To the frightened servant, the whole kit-and-caboodle looks like it is going to King Aram in a handbasket, but Elisha could see a here-and-now that most of us don't always detect. His eyes beheld an outnumbered, outranked, over-whelmed, outgunned, and soon-to-be crushed enemy who is hemmed in on every flank by the colossal armed forces of God who are geared up, standing by, equipped, and prepared to open up a whole can of divine heavenly whoop on Aram's armed, hell-bent battalion. Now I do believe I am more likely to identify with the distressed servant of Elisha when I say that I would have almost certainly fallen victim to blind fear, piddled my pants, thrown in the towel and cried uncle had I caught a glimpse of the good-sized army of ferocious-looking, out-for-blood warriors in their combat-equipped chariots encircling them!

Hebrews 11:1 (NIV) — *"Now faith is confidence in what we hope for and assurance about what we do not see."*

I am sure of what I hope for, and I am certain of what I do not see but truth-be-told sometimes what I see, taste, touch, hear, smell and experience can cause me to act like a one-eyed cat watching two rat holes. I read about the heroes, the great oaks of faith in Hebrews 11 and I can't help but cry out, "Lord take this nut of yours and make her into a great oak. Help me to walk by faith and not by sight!

Hebrews 11 — *"By faith Noah, when warned about things not yet seen, in holy fear built an ark to save his family. By his faith he condemned the world and became heir of the righteousness that is in keeping with faith.*

"By faith Abraham, when called to go to a place he would later receive as his inheritance, obeyed and went, even though he did not know where he

was going. By faith he made his home in the promised land like a stranger
in a foreign country; he lived in tents, as did Isaac and Jacob, who were heirs
with him of the same promise. For he was looking forward to the city with
foundations, whose architect and builder is God.

"By faith Abraham, when God tested him, offered Isaac as a sacrifice.
(There was no alternative sacrifice waiting for Abraham until after He acted
by faith) He who had embraced the promises was about to sacrifice his one
and only son, even though God had said to him, 'It is through Isaac that your
offspring will be reckoned.' Abraham reasoned that God could even raise the
dead, and so in a manner of speaking he did receive Isaac back from death.

"By faith Isaac blessed Jacob and Esau in regard to their future.

"By faith Jacob, when he was dying, blessed each of Joseph's sons, and
worshiped as he leaned on the top of his staff.

"By faith Joseph, when his end was near, spoke about the exodus of the
Israelites from Egypt and gave instructions concerning the burial of his bones.

"By faith Moses' parents hid him for three months after he was born,
because they saw he was no ordinary child, and they were not afraid of the
king's edict.

"By faith Moses, when he had grown up, refused to be known as the son
of Pharaoh's daughter. He chose to be mistreated along with the people of God
rather than to enjoy the fleeting pleasures of sin. He regarded disgrace for the
sake of Christ as of greater value than the treasures of Egypt, because he was
looking ahead to his reward. By faith he left Egypt, not fearing the king's
anger; he persevered because he saw him who is invisible. By faith he kept the
Passover and the application of blood, so that the destroyer of the firstborn
would not touch the firstborn of Israel.

"By faith the people passed through the Red Sea as on dry land; but when
the Egyptians tried to do so, they were drowned.

"By faith the walls of Jericho fell, after the army had marched around
them for seven days.

"By faith the prostitute Rahab, because she welcomed the spies, was not
killed with those who were disobedient.

"And what more shall I say? I do not have time to tell about Gideon,
Barak, Samson and Jephthah, about David and Samuel and the prophets,
who through faith conquered kingdoms, administered justice, and gained

what was promised; who shut the mouths of lions, quenched the fury of the flames, and escaped the edge of the sword; whose weakness was turned to strength; and who became powerful in battle and routed foreign armies. Women received back their dead, raised to life again. There were others who were tortured, refusing to be released so that they might gain an even better resurrection. Some faced jeers and flogging, and even chains and imprisonment. They were put to death by stoning; they were sawed in two; they were killed by the sword. They went about in sheepskins and goatskins, destitute, persecuted and mistreated— the world was not worthy of them. They wandered in deserts and mountains, living in caves and in holes in the ground.

"These were all commended for their faith, yet none of them received what had been promised, since God had planned something better for us so that only together with us would they be made perfect."

Right now, as sure as you and I are sitting here, the earth is spinning on its axis at a speed of over one thousand miles per hour. Get out of the city! And at the very same time, the earth is rotating around the sun at a speed of 66,000 miles per hour. Just the thought makes me dizzy! Thank you, Abba Daddy we can't sense any of it. Yikes! I read that Einstein once made his point about this astonishing speed by hitting two consecutive blows with his fist and saying, "Between those two strokes, we traveled thirty miles." And without any perception of it! But lack of perception does not make it any less true, does it?

A. W. Tozer says, "The world of sense intrudes upon our attention day and night for the whole of our lifetime. It is clamorous, insistent, and self-demonstrating. It does not appeal to our faith; it is here, assaulting our five senses, demanding to be accepted as real and final. But sin has so clouded the lenses of our hearts that we cannot see that other reality, the City of God, shining around us. The world of sense triumphs."

May it not be so in our lives! I want the lenses of my heart to be crystal clear so that I see the truth, the City of God shining all around me. Don't you?

Every time I read 2 Kings 6:8-17 I get yet another glimpse of a truth that I need to take hold of, rest in and act upon. Elisha's unobstructed and splendid eyesight of God's workings was grounded in the fact that he was heeding, taking note of, and listening to God's voice. How else would he have been aware of the undertakings of King Aram! Wow, there is no slack in the God of angel armies' rope for He is more than able to patch up our spiritual sightlessness and deliver us a faith-lift like nothing or no one else ever could. Cross my heart and hope to spit!

Truth-be-told, when it comes to acting upon the truth of our Abba Daddy's word, visual impairment can cripple and blindside us so badly that it causes a spiritual far-sightedness persuasive enough to stop an elephant in its tracks. Just because we don't perceive something doesn't make it not so! Just because we are hard of hearing, unmoved, and unresponsive to God's shouting or his small whisper does not change the fact that He is clearly speaking. Just because we can't see or are unaware of something doesn't mean it's not there. Relying on our perception, perspective, or five senses, which intrude upon our attention day and night, will and can outdo the best of us as well as produce the worst in us if we let it. And maybe it just means that we need to get off our bums and go to the gym of God's truth and start exercising that faith muscle He gave us so that we have eyes to see even when the darkness is blinding and ears to hear even when the silence is deafening. I'm preaching to the choir, y'all.

Our problem is that we permit so much bull to obstruct the existence of His presence in our lives when instead we should be throwing a good ol' fashion Holy Spirit rodeo, taking the bull by the horns, and putting it to death by stringing it up with the belt of truth.

It was the very first day of the grand opening of my quilt and country store at a new location and my husband and I had decided to celebrate by going to breakfast that morning before the store opened. While we were having breakfast, I began to get a strong unexplainable feeling that there was something not quite right at our daughter's house. I had no justification for the impression but knew that in the past when I had felt this very same thing and had acted upon the troubling inklings that my out-of-nowhere promptings had turned out to be spot on. So midway through our special meal, I made quite a few stabs at phoning my daughter only to get no response and most definitely no peace. The sense that there was indeed something life-threatening or crucial taking place with my daughter and my grandchildren just would not dwindle away but in fact, as time passed it only intensified. With the gnawing gut feeling not letting up anytime soon I asked my husband if he would drop by our daughter's apartment and check in on her and our two young grandchildren.

No sooner had I opened the store than I received a phone call from my composed husband. He told me that he was situated in his car in the parking lot of our daughter's apartment and that after making several noisy efforts to get someone to come to her door, no one had answered. This knowledge should have placated my unease and settled down my restless heart but instead, it only caused an even more powerful and unreasonable sense of urgency in my bones so fierce that I could not help but appeal to my levelheaded and unruffled husband to try once more. It was as we were getting ready to end our conversation that my husband happened to glimpse up at our daughter's second-story apartment window and see our grandson's small, weepy, frightened, and innocent face pressed firmly against the windowpane and his small arms upraised and flapping for his grandpa's attention. Seeing our grandson's helpless and pleading face pushed up to the windowpane was all the motivation my husband required to urge him to go back to the apartment door and bang on it forcefully! He was determined to get into her residence any way necessary, even if it meant smashing through a window or door.

As he was banging on the door and shouting loudly for someone to open it and almost on the verge of kicking it in, the door swung open, and he found himself face to face with a mysterious, grubby, spaced-out, heavy-eyed, unhappy, and extremely irritated male. Of course, my husband could not have cared less about intruding upon the unknown inhabitant's siesta as his only worry at that moment was for the well-being of our grandbabies. My husband informed the dazed stranger of his identity and then questioned him as to the whereabouts of our daughter. Without dilly-dallying and clearly ignorant of how protective, riled-up, and immovable the grandfather and father standing in front of him was, the unfamiliar fella treaded to the self-protective side and declared haughtily that our daughter had left him to babysit the kids the day before. My eagle-eyed husband, although he already knew the answer, questioned the child-minder from hell even further by asking him where his grandchildren were. Oblivious to the tight spot he was in and without taking into account how perilous the ground might be that he was staggering upon, the smug stranger then divulged to my husband, matter-of-factly and with indifference, that our grandkids were locked away upstairs in the bedroom and that he was just asked to keep an eye on them, nothing more. My husband, calling upon all the self-control he could muster up to not do bodily harm to the strange man, pushed past the male, and dashed up the flight of steps and to the bedroom where he had last caught a glimpse of the pleading face of our grandson.

What he portrayed to me later that night about the state of our daughter's apartment and the space where our grandbabies were imprisoned still fractures my heart and causes me to shed tears. My sweet man was so messed up and weeping uncontrollably as he described the scene. Our two small grandchildren, who were mere toddlers, had been ambling around an almost stripped-bare and dirty room, with nothing on but their poop and urine-filled diapers while eating tiny cracker crumbs off the floor. When they spotted their Dabado, their devoted, shielding, and caring grandfather, their faces lit up with joy as they lifted their hands to the sky and darted to him. They latched on and clung to him like their very life hinged on him and him alone. He promptly snatched them both up into his caring and protective arms and proceeded back down the stairs. When he got to the bottom of the stairs, he was taken aback to discover the not-so-wise, cocky, and stoned fella waiting for him and all geared up for a squabble. I won't get into the heated exchange that my hubby had with the indifferent, child-neglecting stranger lounging on our daughter's couch, but I will disclose that after a good number of fiery words that my defender and protector of the weak and innocent gave that young man to the count of 10 to get out of Dodge. Any hoot, for the first time since my husband had come into contact with the spaced-out stranger, the not-so-wise babysitter made a very wise choice to make a run for it by speedily jumping on his bicycle and hauling out of there as if the hounds of hell were on his tail.

Words could never, nay ever, thoroughly convey the gravity of our sorrow that we experienced upon discovering our grandbabies in such a dreadful set of circumstances or the excruciating and heartbreaking fear and worry that enveloped us when we couldn't fathom our daughter intentionally doing such a thing.

That heart-rending day the babies came home to our house. By the grace of God, we were able to maintain some level of composure and not lose it in front of them as we fed, bathed, dressed, and thoroughly loved on them until finally, they could no longer keep their little eyes open. After they were tucked in and safe for the night, we began to approach the subject of our daughter and talk about whether she was alive or not. We could not accept as truth that our daughter would or could, on her own volition, leave her children the way she did, and so we ultimately convinced ourselves that she had to be lying hurt or dead somewhere. It was the only assumption that, as her parents, we could conjure up or, truth-be-told, accept.

For three days we waited for her to come home or to call. We were startled every time the phone rang, or someone knocked at the front door. My husband searched any and everywhere he could think of, but he could find no sign of her or any information about her. Nothing! On the fourth day, she was found by the police in a crack house, completely oblivious to the goings-on around her or to her children's precarious predicament. So, there we were, in our early forties, now entrusted with the care of two small toddlers' emotional and physical well-being as well as grieving over the dangerous direction our daughter's life had taken. I can't even commence to describe the emotional and physical stress, nor the thoughts and emotions that go on in your head and your heart and that come crashing down on your life the day you discover and come face to face with the fact that the child you raised is an addict.

Any hoot, the events that unfolded prior to finding our daughter made no never-mind to her because she was so wrapped up in getting money for her next fix. Within a few days after learning that our daughter was an addict, we received a call from the police telling us that she was in jail. We had already come to the unavoidable conclusion that we would eventually be getting a call from either the police or the coroner.

It was right after that that we got a call from our grandson's biological father. He wanted to know if he would be able to pick up our grandson and spend some time with him. Again, everything in my body cried out that something major bad was about to go down again but who was I to deny a father time with his child? Well, he picked up our grandson with the understanding that he would be returning him on a specific day. When the day rolled around for our grandson's father to bring him home, he was a no-show. When we were finally able to reach him by phone, he informed us that he was not bringing our grandson back because he was concerned about what kind of grandparents we might be because we had raised an addict. He then coldly informed us that if we wanted to see our grandson Caleb, we would have to take him to court.

So, there I was once again, shut up to faith, surrounded on all sides, caring for a little girl who could not understand the absence of her mother and brother, fighting for the right to just see and hold our sweet grandson who had to think we didn't want him anymore, while watching on helplessly as our daughter's life hung in the balance.

One night I sat down with my sweet little granddaughter to continue our nightly habit of reading a bedtime story together. The book I was drawn to was one that had been given to me by a dear friend when we first learned that our little Caleb was coming into this world and was titled, "Caleb the Littlest Angel". Well, Caleb the littlest angel had been given by God the very important task of placing a rainbow in the sky to remind everyone that God keeps His promises. However, Caleb felt it was so crucial for us to bring to mind the faithfulness of God that he felt the need to place not one but two rainbows in the sky. A double reminder of the goodness and faithfulness of God. Well don't you know that smack-dab in the middle of my reading the story about this precious little angel who bore the same name as my sorely missed grandson didn't I began to weep like there was no tomorrow. My granddaughter, who was pushing a tad past the age of two, just didn't know what to make of all my carrying-on, just sat there quietly in my lap staring at me with a look on her face that most southerners who are questioning if you missed the brain train are to bound to have when they say, "Bless your heart." It bowled me over when instead of wrapping her arms around me and comforting me she placed her tiny hands over my mouth and quietly said, "Ssssshhh!"

With as much self-control as I could muster, I gently responded, "Baby I just can't stop crying. I miss Caleb!"

With a look of concern for me she tilted her head up as if listening to someone else, then looked at me and she asked ever so softly, "Don't you hear it Gaga?"

"Hear what honey?" I paused to listen, but there was only dead silence.

"Baby I don't hear anything!" The look of surprise and disappointment on her face took me back a bit.

She shook her little head in amazement, placed her tiny toddler fingers to my lips, and with a big all-knowing and confident smile whispered,

"Sssssh! GaGa it's God! He's talking! Listen!"

Taken aback I could only respond with "Oh, baby I can't hear Him!"

Once again, she placed her finger up to my lips, shook her head, and said, "Ssssh, Gaga! Gaga you just be quiet! Stop talking! You just need to listen! Ssssh!"

I listened, y'all, but honest-to-Pete I couldn't hear a thing.

"Oh baby, I just can't hear God. What is He saying?"

A tad-bit frustrated with my hearing problem, she turned her sweet head, as if she was listening intently to someone else in the room, and then she looked back at me with such a sweet tenderness, took my adult face in her small baby hands, and softly whispered, with so much love, joy, and certainty, "Gaga, God says to tell you He loves you!"

So, there I was, surrounded by the enemy, hemmed in by my fears and grief, and shut up to faith, and God, in His sweet and perfect love, used a little child whose heart was open to His voice to remind me that I was not in the battle alone. He didn't tell me everything was gonna turn out the way I wanted it to. He didn't tell me I would see Caleb again. He didn't tell me my daughter was gonna be okay! No, He just reminded me of the one thing I truly needed to know and remember; He loves me and He is with me.

I think that sometimes our faith and trust barometer in God rises and falls based more on what we perceive, feel, or what we can or cannot see more than what we know to be true about Him. I have been guilty of that, I confess.

Fear says you will fall. Fear says the battle is lost! Fear says you won't make it! Fear says you are alone! But like my zip-lining escapade, I've learned that all I need to do is "by faith" step off the platform of my fears into his promises and his faithfulness with my eyes wide open to experience and understand, despite what I feel or the circumstances that surround me that I am not plummeting down to the ground but soaring on the wings of his faithfulness, strength, and power. And trust me, when you do that, you won't be able to do anything but shout, "Woo Hoo"!

Freedoooooooooooooooooooom! Freedom to soar! Freedom to trust! Freedom to find rest in the journey through hills and valleys! Not because you understand it all or because everything is coming up roses or blue-bonnets for that matter, but because we have a God that is bigger than all that is seen and unseen. We need only be still!

We spend so much of our time looking at life from a vantage point that is inaccurate and incomplete. Our perspective of everything is based on what we can see, touch, feel, and understand when it should be based on the One true God that knows and sees all. He has a clear view of each of our lives and He is able more than able, to handle us and yes, even me. Therefore, shouldn't we by faith trust our rock-wielding, giant-slaying, army-commanding, water-parting, storm-calming, death-defeating, star-breathing, worship-worthy, holy, and faithful God when He says I love you and I will never leave nor forsake you!

So, I choose to step off the platform of my doubt and fears into the seen and unseen and trust that no matter what comes my way, He carries me. I choose to have faith, even when I can't see, even when I feel like or perceive that I am surrounded by the enemy, that my Abba Daddy has hedged me in on all sides and I will not be shaken! He is bigger than any giant in my life that may come at me. "My fear doesn't stand a chance when I stand in Your love!" AMEN!

2 Chronicles 20:15-17 — *"Do not be afraid or discouraged because of this vast army. For the battle is not yours, but God's . . . You will not have to fight this battle. Take up your positions; stand firm and see the deliverance the Lord will give you…. Do not be afraid; do not be discouraged. Go out to face them tomorrow, and the Lord will be with you."*

I wrestled with going into the specifics regarding the struggles with our girl. My intention and hope are not to tear her down whatsoever. She has given me permission to talk about this time in our life, as well as to write about it, in the hopes that it may help others. I believe that if things had not unfolded the way they did we would have lost our daughter completely. She has been clean now for well over twenty years. Thank you, Lord!

Be assured that what was intended for harm God meant and used for good. In the midst of our battle, I may have been visually impaired and most definitely deaf, dumb, and blind to God fighting on my behalf! I may not have taken in all the countless things God was doing and the many powerful ways He worked; the discernment that something was wrong, the strength and wisdom He gave us to support and yet not enable our daughter, how He provided a way for us to see our grandson as well as care for our granddaughter, and the women and friends he surrounded us with who showed up at our house to help me bathe and feed the babies. But it never, nay ever, altered the fact that He was by our side and that He loved us thoroughly through it all. I was so far-sighted and night-blinded at times that I lost sight of the God of angel armies who was and is fighting on my behalf. Praiseallujah!

Martin Luther said, "It is in the darkness that we see the stars."

Maybe, just maybe, sometimes we need the darkness for us to get a clear view of the shining light of our loving Father's goodness! Lord, uncloud the lenses of our hearts so that we can see the truth, the City of God, shining around us.

I am so very thankful that my Abba Daddy is not limited by what I see! No matter how dark things have appeared at times, I know it to be an absolute fact and experienced it to be true that the porch light is always burning! He's got me, He's got you, and He's got this!

Psalm 27:13-14 (MSG) —
> *I'm sure now I'll see God's goodness*
> *   in the exuberant earth.*
> *Stay with GOD!*
> *   Take heart. Don't quit.*
> *I'll say it again:*
> *   Stay with GOD.*

The porch light is always burning, even when our eyes can't see! That's the whole hushpuppy. Well at least for now!

CHAPTER SEVEN

ROAD WORK AHEAD

For many years I owned and operated a delightful little quilt and country store. Truth-be-told, it developed into more of a ministry than a business venture, as I can't recall the store ever yielding a profit. Even though the years I spent managing my own business were very demanding most of the time, they were also some of the most noteworthy times of my life and well worth every strand of gray hair.

Well, it just so happened that one day, I became pinky swear sure that God was plainly communicating to me that it was about time for me to roll up the sidewalk, put up the shutters, and bolt the doors to my small business undertaking. Now mind you, I can't fully recall there being a single person, other than my husband, who grasped the revelation I had been given and who was ready to hop on board with the closing or the timing of shutting the store down, but to me it was as plain as a pig on a sofa. I was sure God had, without a shadow of a doubt, placed in my heart and mind a course of action that not only contained a beginning date but an alarming closing date which was only a measly six weeks away.

When I let my landlord in on the God-inspired decision and prompting to close the doors of my business, she was disapproving and dogged in spelling out to me that I was creating a titanic-size blunder. She was whole-heartedly convinced that the time of year and the amount of time I was permitting myself to purge the store's huge inventory was way wide of the mark necessary to successfully sell off all the stock and pay off the debt I had mounted up over the seven years of running the store. I have to say I was a might taken aback by her naysaying attitude as I thought that once she knew that the marching orders were from God, she would be the first to jump on the bandwagon of God's will. I could surmise from the fleeting looks of disapproval and astonishment by many a God-fearing folk that some might be thinking that not only had I lost my vertical hold but that I just might be a few bricks shy of a load.

When the action plan of shutting the doors permanently commenced, we had amassed well over $300,000 worth of inventory as well as mounted up approximately $80,000 in debt. I can't even begin to tally up the number of times I was heavily prodded by well-meaning individuals and friends bent on trying to wrap their heads around the who, where, what, how, when, and in particular, the why of my decision. All I could say, because truthfully there was no strategic plan nor clear-cut line of attack drawn up, was that God had made it crystal clear to me that I was to go out of business, but at no point had He clued me into all the jots and tittles of how the undertaking would unfold.

Now mind you, I didn't have the biblical burning bush or a talking donkey encounter, because I'm pretty sure if I'd had such an experience I would have walked away with my head in the clouds and able to stand up in a court of law and testify to the fact that God has a Texas accent. Just sayin'.

I reckon I'm not gonna piddle down your back and tell you it's raining by admitting that I wasn't about as nervous as a porcupine in a balloon factory and that there were not times when I was as confused as a goat on Astroturf about the means by which I was gonna reach the finish line or even what the final outcome might be. All I can say is that I have been schooled in the truth that God is God, and I am not, so I was heaven-bent on planting my faith in His sovereignty and goodness and unswerving in my doggedness to not run away from His will for my life.

I'm not yanking your leg when I state that I have extensive first-hand knowledge of the fact that it is as easy for me as sliding off a greasy log backward to jack my jaws and ask God to open and close doors in my life. But when the rubber hits the road and zilch is taking place in my life, it's then that I find myself mulling over and questioning whether the lack of movement in my life just might be because I am still clutching, white-knuckled and tightfisted, to the doorknob of the very door I asked God to open or close. Ain't that a hoot! I'm mighty positive that if calluses were to instantaneously materialize on my hands today, baring my inclination to latch on way too tightly to my blueprints and my hankerings, then the palm of my hands would, without a shadow of a doubt, be weighed down with a horde of those thick-skinned piddling nuisances.

Now when God tells you to do something you do it! Right? (We are all squirming in our seats now!) But if we are gonna be authentic in our relationship with our Abba Daddy, we must fess up and acknowledge that there is no fixin' to do something in your sweet time that will ever quite measure up to or compare to doing something at His prompting and in His time. So yes indeedy, I hung out the going-out-of-business sign, prayed I had heard Him right the first time, clung on for dear life, and waited on God to do what only He can and would do.

Well butter my biscuits, don't you know that I was about three extremely long and painful weeks into my not-so-fruitful going-out-of-business sale when a well-dressed man moseyed into my stocked-to-the-rafters store intent on lining his pockets and relieving my distress. After casing the joint and checking out all of the merchandise the overly stocked store had to offer, he slowly shuffled toward the counter where I was stationed, all the while smiling like he had just caught a prize snipe! Once he reached his destination he leaned in and gave me a big snake-oil salesman smile, thoughtfully took a moment to gather his wits and his words before apprising me of the fact that he was ready, willing, and more than able, to purchase my entire inventory, lock, stock, and barrel, at a jaw-dropping steal of twenty cents on the dollar.

Can I just say that I may be ignorant and oftentimes gullible, but I ain't stupid. Bless his heart! Even though I had the intense inkling that he had seen me coming and was trying to rob me blind, I couldn't help but begin to slowly dance between fear and faith as I eyeballed the store which was amply filled to the brim with unsold goods. What-ifs boogied in my head like sugar plums! Of course, with my hesitancy to respond, the pleasant but single-minded man did not help matters much by ripping off the band-aid and brazenly asking me how I thought I was going to get rid of such a large inventory with only three weeks left to the closing deadline. I had no answers! I was only sure of one thing! That God had orchestrated it all and that indeed it would be God who would finish it! I can explain it to you, but I can't make you understand. Shucks, even I didn't understand. I just knew I knew and that's all I know! You know!

I do have to admit that it was plumb scary as all get-out looking around the shop with its mounds of unbought inventory, altogether aware of the hefty amount of debt still unpaid and coming face to face with the reality that in just three weeks' time it would all need to vanish, one way or another. Truthfully, I felt like I was located once again, smack-dab in the middle of another "shut up to faith" situation. So right then and there, before God and the snake-oil salesmen, I elected to be faithful to God's prompting, faithfulness, and power, in spite of the intense knocking of my knees, queasiness in my stomach, and hammering of my heart, which I could only attribute to my nearsightedness. Nervously, because I knew my reply would not make a lick of sense to the salesman, I sweetly smiled at the man as I gingerly (as a redhead I've been waiting to plug that word) and calmly refused his not-so-generous offer. I was compelled to tell him more than he probably needed to know or wanted to hear by revealing to him that God had called me to do it and He would make a way through it! I could tell my answer had left him about as confused as an Aggie trapped in a round room searching for a corner! Sorry Aggies! Of course, being one to not let the door close that easily behind him the persistent man went straight for the jugular and asked,

"How do you know God didn't send me?"

In that moment I kind of related to the moment Eve was confronted by the serpent's question, "But did God really say?" Now mind you God didn't give me all the details, but I knew that however He was gonna move this mountain it would be obvious that it was Him! Honest-to-Pete the man's offer felt more like a trap door, a way out of trusting God rather than a mountain-moving act of God.

And I'm fairly sure you could have knocked him over with a feather after I finished spilling the beans about God's prompting and my willingness to trust in His faithfulness. I suppose he accepted my crazy-for-Jesus attitude and came face to face with the fact that he was barking up the wrong tree and that he had a better chance of haggling with a wooden Indian than a pigheaded woman intent on doing God's will. Or maybe he just reckoned that if my brain was dynamite, I still wouldn't have enough to even blow my nose! It makes no never mind, because he gave me a sympathetic (at least I think that is what the look was) close-lipped smile, turned, and made a hasty bee-line for the store exit. As he was fixin' to leave, he took one last bewildered and nervous look around at the overly stocked store and skeptically declared,

"You sure have a whole lot of faith."

Jiminy Cricket, I was so thankful that he couldn't pick up on my heart pounding or the deafening gulp of fear that I had swallowed at his bald-faced statement that made me doubt if maybe, just maybe, I had sunk my teeth into a little bit more than I could chew!

I was taken aback when instead of opening the door to leave, he sashayed back to the counter with a look that said I didn't know Jack or Jill for that matter, passed me his business card, and matter-of-factly and all-knowingly said, "Give me a call when you get to closing day and need someone to take all this inventory off your hands."

Faster than a knife fight in a phone booth the tussle was over, and I felt like someone had licked the red off my candy! Honest-to-Pete, I staggered through my store, moving way too effortlessly and swiftly, back and forth between what-if-knee-shaking-fear and even-if mountain-moving-faith, praying, crying, and pleading with my God as I laid hands on numerous items in my shop and all the while reminding God that it was all His plan and that I was trusting in Him! By the end of the day, I was battle-weary tired but totally at peace with whatever or however God's plan would unfold.

Even if . . .

Gosh, by golly, I couldn't believe how fast the next three weeks passed as the last day of the store's six-week everything-must-go-now close-out sale finally arrived. I meandered around the store boohooing like a baby! Practically everything had sold like hotcakes, including the fixtures, open sign, and cash register. Even a weather-exposed wooden well planter that had been in the elements for over 7 years sold for a good price. If it wasn't nailed down, it sold! Ain't that a hoot! Honest-to-Pete, I'm pretty sure if there had been a kitchen sink, I would have sold that too! I could hear my footsteps echo on the wooden floor as I strolled into the almost empty section of the store where only the day before mountains of fine-looking quilts had decked out the walls and racks.

As I danced into the previously overstocked quilt room, I was smacked full in the face by the sight of one solitary quilt hanging on the stark-naked wall. Now I fancied and was grateful for the beauty of the majority of the quilts I had brought into the store to peddle and in fact, even knew them by name, but one quilt was as ugly as my grandmother's toenails. U-G-L-Y! Any hoot, it was while I was conveying my thankfulness to God and getting my worship on for the God-sized, mountain-moving wonder I had seen unravel before my prone-to-near-sightedness eyes over the past six weeks, that I commenced to beseech God to liberate the poor unappealing quilt from the dumpster-life and put the finishing touches on what He had begun by bringing someone into the store who would love it, ugly and all, and take it off my hands. Honest-to-Pete, I would have given it away if I could have found someone willing, but up to that point no one had conveyed a hankering for it.

Well, no sooner had I prayed that sentiment, than don't you know the bell above my store entrance door tinkled, announcing that someone was entering. I was a little taken aback as it was almost closing time and the very last day! Thinking it was someone coming to say their farewell, I hurried back to the main room of the store, only to be greeted by a sweet lady that I did not know. Before I could say boo, she enthusiastically let me know that she had just caught wind of the fact that I was going out of business and had one quilt left. Well, butter my butt and call me a biscuit!

I wish that at that moment I had taken a selfie because even I would have liked to have seen the look of complete shock on my face! I was bowled over as all get out and I'm somewhat sure she had to be taking into consideration that I just might be three gallons of crazy in a two-gallon bucket, because instead of welcoming her fittingly I just began to do a happy dance and holler,

"Praise the Lord!", trailed by a lively and inquiring, "Who told you?"

If she had said God, right then and there I would have given up the ghost, hailed my chariot to heaven, and kissed this world goodbye!

But God . . .

works in mysterious ways and doesn't always use the methods we would use. Ain't that hoot. And I'd be perjuring myself if I said I wasn't holding my breath, hanging on to her every word, and trying not to piddle my pants as I waited on her to divulge to me the name of the one who had let her in on the breaking news that we had one quilt left in need of home, albeit unsightly as all get-out. She quickly shared with me that she had been getting her hair done down the road a piece when the ladies there began to chat about my shop closing. Now mind you, instead of quickly ushering her into the next room to see the last surviving quilt in our store before she changed her mind, I did something no valuable salesperson or profit-making business owner worth their weight in gold or silver should ever, nay never, do! I began to stroke her arm and sympathetically as if her cat had died, assure her that yes, I did indeed have one quilt left for the taking, but that it was ugly as homemade sin and almost certainly not what I was sure she could be searching for. Ain't that a hoot! Yep, there are instances when even I question whether there's a tumbleweed in Texas with a higher IQ than mine!

Not eager to give up on her goal that easily, the highly motivated and persistent woman insisted upon seeing the quilt and concluding for herself as to whether or not it was befitting her "taste"! She was beside herself with the hope that her five-year search would soon be over and that maybe she had found the perfect quilt while I, on the other hand, was totally sure she was not going to get any satisfaction that day either!

Half-heartedly, all the while preparing myself for a big fat no, I led the poor woman to the quilt room and to what I was sure was gonna be a big let-down! As we marched to her disappointment, I gave it my best Bluebird try to prepare her by over and over reinforcing the fact that the quilt I had was as ugly as ten miles of bad road. I know! I know! I whole-heartedly braced myself for her gag-reflex reaction I knew was on the horizon as we rounded the corner! When her sweet hope-filled eyes settled upon the unsightly peach-pit quilt, a patchwork quilt of way too many pastel colors, which upset my stomach and caused my eyes to ache, she lit up like a Christmas tree and began to squeal like a pig in mud and proclaim her undying love for the ugly-duckling quilt. She was so happy! She couldn't contain her joy and excitement as she began to spew out all the many reasons why the "quilt nightmares are made" of was indeed the quilt of her wildest dreams! Shucks, I'd hate to know what her nightmares are like! Just sayin'! As it turned out it was also the exact size she needed too! Just take a minute and let that soak in!

On the last day of my store being open, God closed the door to a ride of faith that has and will carry me down treacherous roads and through many valleys of trials for a lifetime. This is our God! At the end of the day, I strolled out of my store, smiling and praising, carrying the only inventory left over from the six-week closeout: one small box of candles. It's the God's honest truth that not only did we sell almost all the store inventory in six weeks without any form of advertising, but we also had ample enough money to pay off all our debt and $20,000 leftover to boot.

I reckon if I had yielded or caved under the pressure of my doubts and fears and others' criticism and near-sighted advice, I would have never grasped or experienced the power of God to take what appeared to be to others a ridiculous and impossible feat and transform it into a God-size, God-revealing, faith-cultivating, mountain-moving, roof-crashing, life-altering God moment. If I had held tightly onto the doorknob of my fears and limited understanding, I would have failed to see God swing doors wide open as well as slam doors shut in such a powerful way. To quote Garth Brooks, "I could have missed the pain, but I would have missed the dance!" And oh what a dance it was. Wowsa! To God be the glory!

I can't help but think about the Israelites! Every time I reflect upon the story of the Israelites in the book of Exodus, I am bowled over by their constant complaining and forgetfulness. Seriously, take a moment to soak in all that God executed and accomplished right in front of their very eyes!

The God of Abraham went so far as to set apart a man named Moses, who at the first howdy was more content to stay in the shadow of his mama's apron than do God's bidding, all because he was more distracted by his inadequacies than focused on God's capabilities.

The God of the universe, the Creator of all that is seen and unseen, opened up a whole can of divine whoop on all those little man-made gods that Egypt bowed down to by beating them like a red-headed step-child right before the Israelites' very eyes.

And how could we forget about that arrogant, mean-as-a-mama-wasp, Pharaoh, with his heart as hard-edged as a cast-iron commode and who could strut sitting down! The God who fights on our behalf displayed for the Israelites who the Great I Am is by flinging that all-gurgle-and-no-guts Pharaoh and his enemies-of-God army about like tumbleweeds in a Texas Tornado.

And then to top off the sundae of God's goodness, God didn't just send off the Israelites on their jolly way into a barren region where it's hotter than a burning bush to grope and stumble amidst the cactus and scorpions alone but He went with them as a pillar of fire by night and a cloud by day. Can you imagine such a thing? A glimpse of the glory of God with you wherever you rest or roam! Ain't that the berries!

I'd be fibbing if I said I wouldn't love to have such a visible spectacle of His power and goodness steering me around each and every day of my life. Can you even begin to conjure up in your mind what that must have been like to encounter? In just a small-scale way it would be like taking a walk-about in the shoes of Pigpen in the Peanuts cartoon, who always has this little cloud of dirt engulfing and trailing him. Shucks, even I could sit still for that! And that's saying a whole heck of a lot. Woo Hoo! The struggle is real!

And I can only begin to imagine what the headlines in the Egyptian Times (if they had such a thing) and across the world might have been on that extraordinary, mind-blowing day of Israel's mass exodus from servitude!

The One True God Makes Himself Known!

Egypt Plagued with Horror as Little G's Exposed as Bogus!

Brick Layer's Union Up in Arms as Mass Exodus Generates a Shortage of Slaves!

Red Sea Splitting Sweet for Israelites/Not So Sweet for Egyptian Army!

I'd like to suppose that the awareness of God's goodness and faithfulness, power, and love must have puffed up the Israelites' confidence in God to such an out-of-this-world magnitude that every Tom, Dick, and Harry felt the tremors of the Israelites' faith reverberating all the way through Egypt and beyond.

I enjoy conjuring up in my mind's eye the eye-popping expressions of awe-struck amazement on their unshackled faces, the giddy joyfulness in their voices as they delivered up, over and over, a news report of God's epic and mind-blowing emancipation of the people He loved.

I like to imagine that they celebrated and danced as they sang praises with unleashed restraint and that they slumped to their faces before the God-that-Saves in out-of-this-world thankfulness as the realization drenched their hearts that the great I Am had taken notice of their cries for a hero and had come to their rescue.

I wonder if they worshipped without restraint and in no-holds barred surrender to the Great I Am as they sang at the top of their voices to Jehovah-Jireh, "I called, you answered, and you came to my rescue!"

Whatever their comeback at the onslaught of being set free, it is clear as glass that fast as small-town gossip, the Israelites, who could have been moving mountains and should have been content as a clam at high tide because they were safer than granny's snuff box in the glorious presence of the Almighty God who journeyed with them day and night, got their panties in a wad and began to moan, groan, and go to pieces like someone who has just found a yellow jacket in the outhouse. Instead of praising, worshipping, and trusting in the God who heeded their cry and freed their lives from 430 years of intense labor, bondage in chains, and servitude, they began to nit-pick, gripe, and squabble. We used to say to our kids when they were having their whining parties, "Would you like some cheese with that whine?"

Well, those Israelites had a whole lot of whine!

"No water Moses?"

"I could have had a V-8, Moses!"

"Leftovers again! Where's the beef, Moses?"

"My feet hurt!"

"Did I shave my legs for this, Moses?"

"Are we there yet, Moses?"

"Did God bring us out here just to die, Moses?"

"I gave up being a slave for this?"

"Moses, we would have been better off if we had stayed in Egypt!"

Honest-to-goodness, their rantings are so woeful that it would bring tears to a glass eye!

In the bat of an eyelid, or should I say in the closing of an eye, the rubbernecking, stiff-necked Israelites failed to recall and opted to forget God's ever-loving faithfulness, almighty power, and presence. Spiritual blindness to the spectacular power and extraordinary goodness of God set in like a debilitating and infectious bug and even though they could unmistakably see and hear that God was with them, they set their sights on the desires of the flesh and exchanged the spectacular for the mundane by melting down their man-made jewelry to form a golden calf to worship. Holy Cow! Or not!

But you and I, well, I'm so thankful we aren't anything like those stiff-necked wanderers! We can get our praise on, jump up and down, and dance as we holler to the rafters about our unwavering faith. Woo Hoo!

We can thank our Father God that we are nothing like those stiff-necked, bellyaching, crabby, miserable, hard-to-please, nagging, ill-tempered, discontented, unseeing, doubters that never whine!

We can throw out a Hallelujah that we have never been shamefaced and guilty of spiritual amnesia or night blindness where we have overlooked, neglected, ignored, or disremembered the lavish watchfulness, holy uprightness, overcoming muscle, gargantuan undertakings, sacrificial, and immeasurable passion and unfaltering faithfulness of our Abba Daddy! Yes!

Praiseallujah that we are nothing like those far-sighted Israelites who fell ill to constipation of thought, diarrhea of the mouth, and all out faithlessness because they were too occupied by the landscape and distracted by the state of affairs about them than they were at relying on and trusting in the God directly in front, beside and all-around them! Amen!

Don't be scared stiff or taken aback if you just experienced the ground shaking as your ears picked up the sound of a deafening thud. It was only me collapsing to my knees in regret and sorrow over the loads of times I have gone belly up by failing to bring to mind and take into account the satisfying goodness of God in my life! For indeed there are moments when I have been no different, no better than those Israelites.

It's funny—not funny ha-ha—how spiritual sightlessness, amnesia, or night-blindness can slink its way into our lives, muddy our minds, and impede our vision of His goodness. Maybe sometimes it's because we want what we want when we want it and when we don't get what we want we moan and pitch a hissy fit-times-four and start gnashing our teeth and getting mad at God when truth-be-told maybe, just maybe, there is something that the Creator of the universe has knowledge of that we just might not and we just need to trust in His goodness and expertise. Ouch!

In fact, just the other day I found a journal from 1999, which I had begun to write in about 3 years after I had given my life to Christ. Wow, reading it was like having a bucket of ice water emptied over my head as the tear-jerking realization soaked into my spirit that I am still, to this very day, praying the exact same prayers for my children that I prayed over twenty something years ago. And I am still waiting . . . The only difference now is that I have added my grandchildren to the list. And yet, even as I write this I realize and am humbled by the fact that there is so much God has done and worked in and through that I never asked Him for. So many things written by His all-knowing and loving hand between the lines of my words.

It's so easy to get enshrouded by the things not seen and seen! Trust me, I know! Truth-be-told, if it were not for the front row seats and backstage passes, I've been furnished to see the goodness of God on display and gushing through the veins of my life over and over then maybe, just maybe, I would have given in to despair and discouragement and disappointment. But I am intimately familiar with and have experienced face to face and personally the truth and splendor of God's goodness. I recognize that even when I don't see the writing on the wall, even though I don't always see Him moving and working in my life, or the lives of others for that matter, that it does not mean that He isn't. It makes me smile and think of the new phrase my grandkids started saying whenever they see a "Road Work Ahead" sign. It drives me crazy and makes me laugh all at the same time, because every time, I kid you not, they see the sign that says "Road Work Ahead" they will in one accord (not a Honda) and Dolby surround-sound shout out, "Road work ahead! I sure hope it does!"

Now it's in your head too! Truth is God doesn't always give us a diagram of the road ahead or the construction looming. He doesn't always warn us of bad road conditions, detours, and delays. But He does give us the map—His word—to help us navigate the road we are on, potholes and all. And He says follow me! And because of the goodness of God, we can know that there is road work ahead and that the road will work! We can bank on it! Woo Hoo!

Recently I sat with one of my grandsons, whose name means bold and faithful, as we gabbed about his deteriorated and tarnished vision of God. He communicated to me that all he needs to believe in the one true God again, the God I love with all my heart, soul, mind, and oomph, is to witness some sort of sign or evidence of Him. This young man, who I love more than words could ever paint, used to have faith that caused mountains to shake in their britches. I kid you not! In days gone by, I would have pinky-swear-promised that one day this young man would most certainly grow up to be the next Billy Graham or D.L. Moody. But somewhere, while traveling along life's road of ups and downs, potholes and detours, exposure to the environment of storms and sunshine, the landscape of hills and valleys, the good and bad drivers, spiritual amnesia, and blindness have taken its toll and his faith in God has declined as his anger at God has increased. Somewhere, he stopped remembering that the God on the mountain is still the God in the valley. (It's funny—not funny ha-ha—how someone can be so angry at a God they say they aren't sure they believe in. Hmmm . . .)

I'm fully mindful to the fact that there are many people who at one point or another in their life have asked the question "Why did God allow this or why didn't God stop this or why didn't God do this?" I'm also aware that when they don't have the answer to those questions, they surmise that God is either not real or not good! Why are we surprised that this earth isn't heaven when God's word so clearly states,

Ecclesiastes 3:1-8 — *"To everything there is a season,*
and a time to every purpose under the heaven:
A time to be born, a time to die;
a time to plant, and a time to pluck up that which is planted;

A time to kill, and a time to heal;
a time to break down, and a time to build up;
A time to weep, and a time to laugh;
a time to mourn, and a time to dance;
A time to cast away stones, and a time to gather stones together;
a time to embrace, and a time to refrain from embracing;
A time to get, and a time to lose;
a time to keep, and a time to cast away;
A time to tear, and a time to sew;
a time to keep silence, and a time to speak;
A time to love, and a time to hate;
A time of war, and a time of peace."

I'm no scholar but could it be that the two questions we should be posing when the storms of life roll in, when the road isn't clear, the weather is treacherous, or traveling gets tough are; "Who is God in all this!" And in light of Who He is, not what I feel, see, or understand, "What should I be doing!"

Truth-be-told, the devil aspires to and hankers for us to stumble around in hopelessness, oblivious, and blind to the light of the world, all the while conducting ourselves in the same manner as an ostrich with its head fixed in the sand. We are the bullseye in his crosshairs, and his topmost aim is to render us barren, fruitless, and of no use in the King-dom of God. Shucks, I can tell you from experience that when I am wallowing in the muck and mire of my disappointments and pain, my circumstances and fear, my doubts and insecurities, and giving in to my spiritual amnesia or night blindness that I am as about as handy as a steering wheel on a mule or a trap door on a canoe!

Honest-to-Pete, I have been injured and broken-down in a manner that I could not have thought possible and by folks I would have never voted most likely-to. I am very conscious of the actuality that I've got way too much sand in my hair and drawers from ducking my head in the sand. In the firestorm of the past few years, I have stopped and dropped out of fear. And instead of rolling in His goodness and faithfulness to walk through the waters and pass through the fires with me, I just may need to confess that I have been guilty of being a tad gun shy and have curled up in what I thought to be a safe place and remained there for a good while. All in a futile effort to shield my wounded and weary heart. God and I have had some major conversations about my traveling problems. Cross my heart and hope to spit!

A couple of years ago, my husband and I were settled into our basement watching television when we heard a loud boom. My husband and I combed the first two floors of the house to see if something had fallen off the walls, but we just couldn't find the cause of the loud noise. So, we went back downstairs and resumed watching television. It wasn't till 45 minutes later when we headed up to our room on the third floor that we ascertained that someone had fired a bullet into our upstairs bedroom. The police were called, and a kind officer came out to investigate the crime scene straightaway. After the officer did what was required for his report upstairs, we proceeded back downstairs to answer further questions. While we were talking with the officer, another loud bang rang out throughout the house. My husband and the officer both recognized it as another gunshot being fired. The officer gave us instructions to go to the basement of our house and then began calling for backup as He rushed out of the house and in the direction of the sound of the second shot. It wasn't till later, when the officer came back to tell us that they had encountered the shooter, that we learned that the second shot had also invaded the privacy of that same bedroom, through the very same wall, and close by to the entry point of the first bullet. As it turned out, the reprobate was our next-door neighbor who had gotten stupid drunk, fabricated his own gun, and chose to test it out by shooting it into the air, not once mind you, but twice.

But God . . .

A few minutes before the startling sound of the first shot interrupting the night, my husband had asked me if I was going to bed because I was nodding off as I often do near bedtime. But as soon as he suggested that I hit the hay, I was overcome by a strong sense of uneasiness and a prompting in my spirit to stay put and not go upstairs. So, I stayed.

When the first shot was delivered, I should have been in our bedroom, and if I had, based on where the bullet entered and the time it was fired, it was more than likely I would have been shot. When the bullet entered our home, it didn't just pass through a wall and exit out another. It came through the side of the bedroom wall where I routinely rested my head and then ricocheted about the room, ultimately landing on the floor on the opposite side of the room. The second bullet, although it had entered from the same direction and through the same wall, took on a slightly different flight pattern as it ricocheted around the room, then up and into our ceiling, never to be found.

I can't even begin to express how peace-shattering, fear-inducing, and unnerving the whole incident was. It took several months for me to be able to walk into our bedroom alone, and even then, I could not compel myself to turn on a light, because the darkness felt safer. It can be so easy, convenient, and comfortable to just bury yourself in the emotions of difficult and trying circumstances. Emotionally blinded to the critical information, that God is good, we are never alone, and He is working for our good in all the good, bad, and ugly things, we end up in a rut, which amounts to a grave with two open ends. The cure for our grave predicament just might be that we need to don our night-vision goggles of truth and take a much closer look, not at our circumstances but at the One Who knows our circumstances. Focusing on the truth of Who He is and not on our state-of-affairs is what will set us free and give us ears to hear and eyes to see. Sometimes we just don't see the evidence because we are so jammed up in the physical that we can't see the spiritual.

As I gaze back in astonishment at the accounts of the goings on in my life over the past twenty-seven years, I can't refute the plain truth, that the goodness of God was and is always running after me. His merciful and loving fingerprints can be found on every story told and those yet to be disclosed. I am blessed that in hindsight I can look back in the rearview mirror and clearly see that even when there were bad roads, careless drivers, lousy weather, potholes, detours, collisions, and delays, He was there guiding, protecting, and directing me over and through every joyous and painful mile.

As you've traversed through the pages of this book with but a few stories of my journey, my prayer is that you have caught sight of the unending faithfulness of God displayed in gargantuan ways. I have given you only a glimpse, a back-seat view of my journey, and truth-be-told there is so much more that could be said. Indeed, there are many more places we could travel down the road and explore but for now, this is where our journey ends.

But God . . .

can take what we believe to be a dead end and turn it into a new beginning! My daughter and I have been on the road together several times. What an adventure and a laugh! Inevitably, because we are too much alike, we always get lost or end up going down a road that causes me to question if we are gonna suffer a torturous death by a hungry grizzly, a chainsaw toting maniac, or a psychopathic clown with a red balloon! She cracks me up because her go-to phrase whenever I am sure we are lost or doomed to a horrific death in the boondocks is, "All roads lead to somewhere, Mommy!"

In God's all-knowing, all-powerful hands, all roads lead to some-where! Even if our vision is limited, our understanding is limited, and our driving a hot mess. I admit that I have days where I forget—or maybe it's more like I choose not to remember—that all my days are filtered through the loving fingers of His grace and are held in His more than capable tender hands.

I have had days where I can't get past the disappointment of the detours, delays, bad road conditions and have allowed hopelessness to pitch a tent in my heart when what I should have been doing all along was donning the garment of praise and shouting hallelujah that His mercy never—nay ever—fails and that He has come to my rescue over and over and over and over and over again and again, even to death on a cross.

I have had days where I have slammed on the brakes, gotten stuck in the muddy, life-sucking rut of my fear and disappointments when what I should be doing is dancing on that foul-smelling grave of lies instead of taking a siesta on the tombstone.

I have had days where circumstances, feelings, and bad drivers claw at my heart and I throw a pity party times four, raise a ruckus, order the cheese and whine, and wallow and fuss when what I should be doing is relishing in my Abba Daddy's faithfulness that has steered me through the fire and water and unknown roads of life more times than I can count and almost certainly more times than I even recognize or know.

I have had days where I am so dry bone-tired weary and discouraged from waiting for the light to change. Days spent praying and waiting, waiting and praying, only to catch a tiny glimpse of the answer to the cries of my heart! It's then that I realize what I need to do is rest in the God's honest truth that He is the God who opens doors only He can open and shuts doors only He can shut. I need to recall the truth that unless and until God shuts the door, it ain't over!

I have had days when sadness and frustration and hurt taunt me to give up, run, and hide far away from everyone and everything. And if I am going to be honest, why stop now, I have had days where I have done just that! Yes, I have been in a place of darkness, weary of my circumstances, broken-hearted, lost, and feeling alone, failing to recall the truth of His goodness, and yearning for a cave to hide away in all because I chose to focus on the road conditions, what I don't have, and what I think I need or want instead of positioning these weak and limited-vision eyes on the satisfying goodness and ever-loving faithfulness of my Abba Daddy.

Recently someone texted me and said that they wanted to be happy, carefree, and perky like me. They wanted to know how I do it. I couldn't help but chuckle as I and God alone truly know the wacky goings-on in this crazy head of mine and the many tears spilled by my sensitive and easily broken heart. I am not always happy, ask my husband, but when I choose to place all my sorrows in His hand and trust in the goodness of God and not my circumstances, feelings, or my limited vision for that matter, I can't help but smile, despite the grieving, and dance with joy in the presence of His goodness, faithfulness, and love.

It's funny—not funny ha-ha—how much of our life we waste on things that won't mount to a hill of beans when one day we find ourselves smack-dab, face to face with the goodness of God. For so many years, I relied on so many things to find my hope, strength, and worth in. For so many years, I ran through the darkness, content to do so, in my blindness bumping and groping along the walls when all I ever needed to do was to turn around and behold the goodness of God running after me.

Traveling to Israel and walking in the very place where the goodness of God came down and pitched a tent among us had an effect on me that I didn't see coming. Before we hop along this bunny trail of the wind-swept meanderings of my heart, would you please take a moment to make the mental or physical note, if you haven't already, that I, Kathy Bowers, am by no means flawless nor have I ever claimed to be. As the ramblings of my mind and grapplings of my heart have unfolded onto these pages, I am woefully and repentantly aware that knowing and doing are two different things. I can climb aboard the train of thought Paul spilled out when He meekly and mournfully acknowledged that "The things I want to do I don't, and the things I don't want to do I do . . ." But more than that I feel like I can, in some small measure, understand and relate with the prophet Isaiah when He was so humbled by the presence of God's glory and holiness that he could do nothing else but fall before Him and profess, "Woe, I am a man of unclean lips."

For I have, with awed impatience and controlled anticipation, journeyed through the streets of a little town called Bethlehem where "The Alpha and the Omega", "The Beginning and the End", "The Bread of Life", "The Word Who is God", "The King of Kings" willingly came down so that He could be swaddled in baby flesh and lie in a feeding trough not worthy nor in keeping with a King's position, let alone the very Son of God.

For I have lingered and worshipped at night, on the dark and stormy shore of the Sea of Galilee, mesmerized by the lightning all about, exhilarated as the rain splashed my face, fearless as the thunder shook the sky, and holding my breath with childlike anticipation as I looked upon the same tempestuous waves that were once calmed by "The Lion of the tribe of Judah," "Who has been given all authority in heaven and on earth."

For I have adored Him with uninhibited, exhilarating, joyful wonder, and awe while standing in a boat floating on the waves of the Sea of Galilee's unpredictable waters where the holy feet of the "Mighty God" strolled.

For I have dipped my feet contemplatively into the Jordan River where our "Wonderful Counselor", our "Hope" was once immersed. Where God announced, "This is My Son in Whom I Am well pleased!"

For I have curiously sauntered through a small piece of the town called Nazareth, which had a reputation for nothing good coming from it, knowing that this seemingly insignificant town with its blemished reputation is the very place in which "The Author and Perfecter of our faith" studied; "The Son of the Most High" prayed and "The True Vine" grew just so He could die for me.

For I have lingered and longed to stay behind in the upper room where the "Lord of All", the "Beloved Son of God", "the Holy One", bathed the soiled feet of His disciples, all the while knowing that one would betray, another deny, and all would abandon Him.

For I have nervously prayed and shed tears of remorse in the Garden of Gethsemane where our "Advocate" and "Good Shepherd", our "Mediator" implored His disciples to stay awake with Him as He earnestly and agonizingly, to the point of sweating blood, prayed for deliverance from a death none of us could possibly imagine and that He most certainly did not earn.

For I have gently ran my hand along the contours of an olive tree believed to be dated back to the time of Jesus and cried as I grasped fully that it was there, in the Garden of Gethsemane (which means oil press), that the spirit of God (which is often symbolized by oil) must have been so crushed as the "Son of God" was bound, betrayed, and abandoned.

For I have ambled in comfort and ease, content, happy, and rested along the stony path where "He Who Knew No Sin" trudged, all the while in excruciating pain from being flogged and beaten beyond recognition. Where "He Who was Faithful and True" was exhausted and weak, stumbled and fell. Where "Our Redeemer" and our "Hope" Who was mocked as a crown of 1-2 inch thorns was placed upon His head. Where our "Messiah" willingly subjected His entire being to unimaginable anguish and torment as He carried my well-deserved 80 to 110-pound cross to the Place of the Skull, Golgotha.

For I have stood in stunned silence as I looked upon the area where He died and pondered what kind of love is this that would choose to be separated from the Father so that sinners, enemies of God, would never have to be separated from Him again.

For I have shared in communion, a time of remembrance of Jesus' body being broken for me and His blood being spilled out, at the Garden tomb, near the place where my filthy rags of sin nailed "The Sacrifice for our sins", the holy, ever-loving, merciful, and innocent precious "Lamb of God" to a wooden cross that was situated between two thieves.

For I have looked upon the place where He willingly bled out His great love for me and I have stood at an empty tomb and sobbed as I thought about the "Resurrection and the Life," "The Way," "The Truth," "The Life," "The Light of the World" being enclosed in darkness upon a cold slab, not because He deserved any of it, but because I had earned every bit of it.

For I have touched a stone like the one that would have sealed His tomb and been reminded that even with all its weight of two to four thousand pounds it was ineffective and unable to stand against "The Door," "The Resurrection and the Life," "The Rock," our "Risen Lord."

When we were at the garden tomb praising God and taking communion, the pastor opened up the time to anyone who would like to share about their joy in the Lord. It was there that I was able to share with people I hardly knew about God hearing my cry one night as I lay crumpled upon a bathroom floor, longing to die, and crying out for help. It was there, at that Garden Tomb, that I ended my testimony by declaring that because He lives, I can face tomorrow! And it was there, just as I said those words that a group across the garden from us began to sing the song, "Because He Lives, I Can Face Tomorrow!"

For all my life I have lived in the goodness of God! But sometimes I have been guilty of not seeing, acknowledging, or basking in it.

God is so good, and it is funny—not funny ha-ha—how He can put just the right words in our mouths for us to relay to others while at the same time, taking us to church by delivering up a message we need to hear. In sharing with my sweet grandson about the many places that I have seen the evidence he says he searches for; the spiritual signs of God in his life that he is so physically blind to, the goodness of God running after him relentlessly even in the most terrible and hurtful of times of His young life I realized that even though I have seen the goodness of God in my life over and over and over again, I have been guilty more times than I could shake a stick at of reacting to my circumstances more than I have been guilty of responding out of the truth of His goodness. All because I failed to remember His sweet love, protection, and power.

1 Samuel 7:1-12 New American Standard Bible (NASB) — *"While Samuel was sacrificing the burnt offering, the Philistines drew near to engage Israel in battle."* The Israelites went out to do battle against the enemy, and God sent them supernatural help: *"That day the LORD thundered with loud thunder against the Philistines and threw them into such a panic that they were running scared before the Israelites" (verse 10).*

To remember the God empowered victory, "Samuel took a stone and set it up between Mizpah and Shen. He named it Ebenezer, (which means stone of help) saying, '*Thus far the LORD has helped us*'" (verse 12).

From then on, every time an Israelite saw the stone raised by Samuel, he would have a reminder of the Lord's power and protection.

We don't have to ask or hope that the road before us works. We have all the evidence we need in the Person of Jesus, that God loves us, and that the road ahead will work because He has paved the way and we do not travel it alone. If we will just open our eyes and see all the stones of remembrance in our life, we will get the best seat in the house and the best lane on the road to God's power, love, and protection on display in a truly magnificent and glorious way.

Kathy Bowers, Age 17, Broken and Lost, Separated from the goodness of God!

I dream of dreams
Of fairy Tales coming true
Of a knight in shining armor
To carry me off into the blue
But here comes reality and there go the dreams
There should be more to life it seems
There are no dreams of the real world
No fairy tales coming true
Only the dream of foolish young girls
With nothing but dreaming to do
Do dreams come true
Or do they Just fade away
Did my Knight in Shining Armor

Get lost along the way.

Tell me There is more to this World than I've Seen

And I just might, Start Dreaming again. (By Kathy Bowers)

> We must not forget the goodness of God that turns our bondage into freedom!

Kathy Bowers, Age 37, Set Free and Alive by the goodness of God!

> We must not forget the goodness of God that turns our mourning into dancing!

Kathy Bowers, Age 60, Basking in the goodness of God!

> We must not fail to recall the goodness of God that turns the darkness into light.

The power of God that takes the mundane and makes it spectacular!

I have traveled so far, not because I have it all together, but because in Him I have found it all!

I have traveled so far, not because I am good, but because He is good. He is my God, my King, my Abba Daddy, and He loves me far beyond words could ever express.

I have traveled so far, not because I always see the truth, but because I know the Truth! That no matter what I see, feel, or experience, the goodness of God is running after me. I don't have to guess if the "Road Works Ahead" for I have seen stone upon stone of God's faithfulness paving the way all my life.

I have come so far because He is God and He is so good! The road works ahead because my God goes before me, and He will fight on my behalf.

Psalm 27:13-14 (NKJV) —

> *I would have lost heart, unless I had believed*
> *That I would see the goodness of the LORD*
> *In the land of the living.*
> *Wait on the LORD;*
> *Be of good courage,*
> *And He shall strengthen your heart;*
> *Wait, I say, on the Lord.*

ABOUT THE AUTHOR

A native of the grand ol' country of Texas, KATHERINE BOWERS, left her blessed country over thirty-nine years ago and now resides in Pennsylvania with her extremely patient and loving husband, Robert. She is the mother of two and Gaga (grandmother) to seven. She has been known as an author, speaker, baker, ship-lap queen, but most of all she identifies as a daughter of the King who is head over heels, soul, mind, heart and oomph, in love with Jesus. Woo Hoo! She is the author of *Spiritual Laxative for the Constipated Soul* as well as *You Don't Dig for Water Under the Outhouse.* Her Bombeckesque style of writing, coupled with her brand of "Texanese," generously seasoned with her humor, quick wit and unforgettable tales of her painful and sometimes humorous past serves up spiritual truth in "bite-sized" nuggets creating a "spiritual tonic "for the aching soul. She has an Associate's Degree in "Life in the Pit," a Bachelor's Degree in "Amazing Grace," and a Master's Degree in "Christ's Redeeming Love." Her hope is to give those travelling this road of life a glimpse of what it really means to be "a blood-bought, battle-fought, saved-by-amazing-grace, daughter of the King.

www.ingramcontent.com/pod-product-compliance
Lightning Source LLC
Chambersburg PA
CBHW010857090426
42737CB00020B/3398